For Father Francis –

With regards & esteem

Malcolm

HATS in the RING

HATS

☆ *in the*

RING

by Malcolm Moos and Stephen Hess

Random House

for Barney

ACKNOWLEDGMENTS

The impetus for this volume comes from ten half-hour films that were prepared in 1956 for the National Educational Television and Radio Center. Our first vote of appreciation, therefore, rightly belongs to Robert Hudson and Donald Hillman of NETRC and our producer, John McGiffert, now producer of "Camera Three."

The unsung heroes of any book are those who must deal with the authors' disorder. No words in *Roget* can fully express our gratitude to two valiant secretaries and decipherers of illegible handwritings: Audra Carter and Polly Sedlak. The people at Random House who cheerfully worked with another form of our disorder were Jess Stein, Charles Lieber, and Leonore Hauck.

If some new enthusiasm, insight, and knowledge have crept into this book, among the many who deserve credit are Arthur Krock, Alistair Cooke, Thomas O'Neill, Robert Donovan, James Reston, Earl Mazo, E. W. Kenworthy, Roscoe Drummond, Walter Lippmann, Russell Baker, Max Freedman, Merriman Smith, and Sidney Hyman.

Several old friends have again come to our rescue.

Among them are Ralph Goldman, Paul David, Richard Bain, Charles Clapp, Eugene Sekulow, and Alvin Deutsch.

Especially grateful are we to those who were always on hand to supply a missing date or a particularly elusive fact—Floyd McCaffree, William Prendergast, Robert Oshins, Richard Scammon, Alexander Heard, and Madlyn Fitzgerald.

In gathering the political cartoons, we have been fortunate in obtaining understanding assistance from Milton Kaplan, Curator of historical prints at the Library of Congress. All of the cartoons by Clifford E. Berryman, William A. Rogers, G. Y. Coffin, and C. J. Taylor are from the Library of Congress collection. We are further indebted to the following cartoonists for generous permission to reproduce their works: Hy Rosen, Albany *Times Union;* and Daniel R. Fitzpatrick, St. Louis *Post-Dispatch*.

Finally, the real silent sufferers are the authors' wives—To Tracy and Elena, our love and thanks.

Malcolm Moos
Stephen Hess

Washington, January 14, 1960

CONTENTS ☆ ☆ ☆

HATS in the RING

☆ ☆ ☆ *The Long Arm of the People's Choice*

"Just wait," explained a newsman to an English visitor impatient for the fireworks to begin at Madison Square Garden in 1924, "those are the Democrats down there."

Rarely could our presidential nominating system be described as pallid politics. It may be clumsy, but it is seldom dismal; it may irritate, yet few can be indifferent.

Who will deny it? "There is something about a national convention," as H. L. Mencken wrote in a frolicsome mood, "that makes it as fascinating as a revival or a hanging. It is vulgar, it is ugly, it is stupid, it is tedious, it is hard upon both the higher cerebral centers and the *gluteus maximus,* and yet it is somehow charming. One sits through long sessions wishing heartily that all the delegates and alternates were dead and in hell—and then suddenly there comes a show so gaudy and hilarious, so melodramatic and obscene, so unimaginably exhilarating and preposterous that one lives a gorgeous year in an hour."

Behind this passionate pageant is the long, winding, twisting story of how America selects her presidents.

This little volume is built upon this unfolding drama.

It takes the reader backstage into the densest cigar smoke of the caucus room and through the snowdrifts of New Hampshire, where every fourth year the "open season" begins with the first presidential primary.

It is a story of false starts and photo finishes; of boomlets and bandwagons; of that lovable equine, the "dark horse"; and of the inevitable broken friendships, bruised prestige, and sometimes even shattered bodies encountered along the precinct trail.

Here is something of the men who made our presidential nominating system what it is; and of those who also ran; of the "men behind the men"—the kingmakers; of the changes that 129 years have wrought; and of the institutions that have resisted time and change.

Among presidential conventions, we readily admit

to having favorites. We hasten to deny that these preferences are prejudices, for certainly no one is hurt by our little foibles. Like the Madwoman of Chaillot, who every morning rereads the same old newspaper and always cries and laughs at the same stories, we are disposed to sympathy when we recall Horatio Seymour, weeping after the Democrats nominated him in 1868 and sobbing to a friend, "Pity me, Harvey, pity me!" Perhaps it is the candidate's name that amuses us; perhaps we feel as we do because poor Horatio seemed so genuinely opposed to running for President.

We cherish the memory of the Alabama delegation standing fast through the longest political convention in history. There is something wondrously loyal about this dedication to a hopeless candidacy. Intoned with a richly waxed Southern accent on each of one hundred and three roll calls at the 1924 Democratic Convention, the name Oscar W. Underwood stands permanently enshrined in the lore of convention craft.

We chanted with the packed galleries, "We want Willkie"; we paraded with our placard, "I Like Ike." We cheered one of the greatest of all nominating speeches—the one that ended "Victory is his habit: The Happy Warrior, Alfred E. Smith." Even Republican hearts skip a beat when the band strikes up "HAPP-y days are HERE again! THE skies a-BOVE are CLEAR again!" We are astonished when we think of a dark-horse nominee like Harding. We take pride in an institution that bestows its highest honor on a defeated senatorial candidate, Abraham Lincoln.

In short, this book is a salute to a quadrennial event in our lives. We do not claim the system is perfect. We know it isn't. No doubt Irvin Cobb was right when he wrote that political conventions represent "more wasted energy, more futile fruitless endeavor, more useless expenditure of noise, money, and talent than any institution on earth."

Yet somehow, above the cosmic din of bizarre demonstrations and pontificating politicians, a choice is made and, by and large, a good one. And so it is that we can all cheer the comment of the *London Economist* on the 1952 presidential nominations: "The great strength of the American system, for all its turbulence, is that the long arm of the people's choice can go deep into the barrel and pull out the best men available. . . ."

Behind the shenanigans, the capers, the honky-tonk, and the carousing, the convention delegates are performing society's most serious mission: perpetuity. They are resolving the succession of leadership.

Much can be learned about a nation from studying its method of recruiting leaders and the way in which power is passed on from one man or group to another. In certain primitive groups, leadership is determined by physical strength or skill. Today one of the most primitive peoples in the world—the aborigines of Melville Island—choose their leader simply by selecting the best hunter in the tribe. In a monarchy, of course, leadership succession is determined by heredity. In some parliamentary bodies, it is a product of seniority.

All these methods have an orderly design. What of leadership succession in a dictatorship? How did Khrushchev rise to power, and what will happen when he dies? Actually, we know very little about how leadership is structured in the Soviet Union. In fact, one of the greatest uncertainties in dealing with Russia is that we cannot know when its leader will be succeeded, who will replace him, and how these factors will change policy.

In the United States, the presidential nominating convention and the general election give us a workable and peaceable system of leadership succession. Yet despite the simple rules of the convention itself, the route to the presidential nomination is a highly complex one, for the nominating process is far more than a meeting every fourth year. The convention is just the periodic climax to a never-ending maze of political operations on all levels—national, state, county, ward, and precinct. And trying to follow the path of a nomination is almost as difficult as trying to nail currant jelly onto the wall, as Theodore Roosevelt once remarked in another context.

It's no surprise that George Washington was not nominated by party convention, for the nation's founders did not even foresee political parties. If the party system has a birthday, some contend that it should be New Year's Eve, 1793. On that date Thomas Jefferson resigned from Washington's cabinet—following the persistent accumulation of factional differences with Alexander Hamilton. Soon thereafter, it became apparent that the nation would choose sides in selecting a chief executive.

By 1800, a method of making nominations was borrowed from the state legislatures. It was known officially as the Congressional Caucus and popularly as "King Caucus." Under this system, a joint session of party members from both houses of Congress selected four presidents of the United States—Adams, Jefferson, Madison, and Monroe.

Later, an attempt was made to make "King Caucus" more equitable by including special delegates to represent districts held by the opposition party. But when the caucus handled Andrew Jackson roughly in 1824, "Old Hickory" used his influence to undermine the system; when he was nominated again in 1828, it was by a combination of "State legislative caucuses, public meetings, and irregular conventions of the people."

Now the ripe moment had arrived for the introduction of the presidential nominating convention.

First to adopt it was the most curious political party the United States has ever known. It all began in 1826 when a gentleman named William Morgan disappeared in upstate New York. Allegedly Morgan was about to publish a book exposing the Masons and his removal had been carefully planned. This rumor exploded existing prejudices about secret Masonic rites and led to the foundation of the Anti-Mason Party, very likely our first third party.

At any rate, the Anti-Masons held the first national nominating convention in Baltimore in 1831. That year, in a building called the Athenaeum, they nominated a former attorney general, William Wirt of Maryland. When the party carried only Vermont in the general election, it quickly evaporated into history. But the following year, the same building saw the first convention to produce a winner. Some 243 Democratic delegates with 103 alternates came to Baltimore to nominate Jackson.

Many customs sprang up at this first major party convention that have persisted over the years. The rule requiring a two-thirds vote to win a nomination was adopted here—a rule that precipitated bitter fights at Democratic conventions for over a hundred years until it was abolished in 1936. Even the tradition that the chairman of the delegation casts the vote of the entire delegation started in 1832. In those days, however, the method of selecting delegates was far more casual than it is today. Some who came to Baltimore were appointed by state party committees, some were chosen by mass meetings, and a few delegates actually appointed themselves.

It was 80 years from the first convention to the famous scene of political carnage that Mr. Dooley described as "a combination iv th' Chicago fire, St. Bartholomew's massacre, the battle iv th' Boyne, the life iv Jesse James, and th' night iv th' big wind." Yet the only basic change that separated the Democratic convention of 1832 and that historic Republican convention of 1912 was the introduction and widespread use of the presidential primary.

Since that day when Theodore Roosevelt stood at the Armageddon, both parties have instituted apportionment reforms, institutionalized the acceptance speech, exalted the public-opinion poll as a political tool and as an instrument of political intelligence, learned the new techniques of public relations and advertising, and tailored their proceedings to radio and television. Yet these are merely refinements—a slightly longer tailfin on last year's model, a little more chrome on the grill. The basic motor remains the same. What other institutions in American life can make this claim?

BORN TO COMMAND.

OF VETO MEMORY.

HAD I BEEN CONSULTED.

KING ANDREW THE FIRST.

In 1832 Andrew Jackson was the nominee of the first major presidential convention and went on to become the first convention nominee to win the presidency.

☆ ☆ ☆ *Paths to the Nomination*

Among the many lessons learned at mother's knee, one of the oldest is the familiar belief that every young man can grow up to be president. But one thing that mother may have forgotten is that to win the presidency, you have first to win the nomination. And there are many paths leading up to that exalted moment on the rostrum when the convention chairman introduces the wildly cheering delegates to "The Next President of the United States."

Presidential contenders have frequently been exposed to the boisterous currents of politics at a tender age. None, though, will probably ever surpass the record of President Martin Van Buren, who was born in a polling place.

Belonging to a well-known political family doesn't hurt presidential ambitions either. Charles Francis Adams, son and grandson of former presidents, looked like the favorite to win the nomination at the Liberal Republican convention of 1872, but the sixth ballot brought a stampede to Horace Greeley and Adams was denied the chance to follow in his ancestral footsteps.

In 1888, the Republicans nominated Benjamin Harrison of Indiana, a great-grandson of a signer of the Declaration of Independence and a grandson of "Old Tippecanoe," President William Henry Harrison. Suspecting the Republicans of trying to cash in on an illustrious name, the Democrats campaigned on the slogan "Grandpa's pants won't fit Benny."

Franklin Roosevelt, of course, had a distant cousin (Teddy Roosevelt) in the White House. But his initial exposure to the presidency is said to have taken place when on a visit to the White House with his father, he was introduced to President Grover Cleveland. The President, harried by the mounting burden of the office, is reported to have told the little boy, "I hope young man you may never grow up to be President."

Several nominees showed an early interest in the presidency. While Robert LaFollette was still in college, a group of friends organized a dollar-a-month club to make him the president of the United States.

This was continued long into LaFollette's career. Although he never became president, he did become a presidential nominee in 1924 on the Progressive Party ticket.

Woodrow Wilson began talking and writing about the presidency while a graduate student at Johns Hopkins University. Years later when he won election, he went to visit an old aunt who was almost totally deaf. She asked her nephew how he was now employed, and he bellowed into her ear trumpet that he had been elected president. "Of what?" inquired the old lady. "Of the United States," Wilson shouted back. "Don't be silly," said the aunt, dismissing the President-elect.

One of the persistent mores of American politics is the snugly-held conviction that a man should not try too hard to be president, that he should be a little coy, a little reluctant. This theory is a carry-over from the idea that the job seeks the man. The belief that a calculated obstinance will pull off a nomination has some basis if one's fellow contestants continue to eat each other up. But it certainly produces some odd dodges and disavowals as eager candidates try not to appear to be seeking the nomination with "the humourless calculation of a certified public accountant in pursuit of the Holy Grail," as an English newsman once put it.

How reluctant can a candidate be and still win a nomination? This brings to mind at once the question of whether a man can be genuinely drafted for the nomination. On this matter opinion divides. The classical instance of "unavailability" is the telegram that William Tecumseh Sherman sent to the Republican convention of 1884. The wire stated firmly, "I WILL NOT ACCEPT IF NOMINATED AND WILL NOT SERVE IF ELECTED." Any candidate who is more equivocal than this is presumed to be hedging and not as reluctant as he appears. But as a postscript to the Sherman telegram it deserves to be noted that the convention was not seriously considering him and that it was his brother John, a former Senator from Ohio, who was the real contender for the nomination.

Through the years, many claims have been made that three presidential candidates were genuinely drafted. First was the unenviable Horatio Seymour —badly defeated by Grant in the general election. So bitter was his opposition to the idea of running for President that the Democratic convention of 1868 quickly adjourned after his nomination so that he would not have a chance to refuse.

The next reluctant candidate was Charles Evans Hughes, a Supreme Court justice at the time of his nomination. Three denials of candidacy were issued by Hughes—"I cannot permit the use of my name." But while he felt deeply that the business of the Court should not be mixed with presidential politics, he could not bring himself to say "no" in the General Sherman formula. After the Republicans made him their candidate in 1916, he immediately resigned from the Court.

In 1952, the country again followed the denials of a candidate for clues as to how reluctant he really was. After repeated preconvention disavowals, Adlai Stevenson was interviewed by a reporter on the eve of the Democratic convention:

"Would you, sir, if the thing became deadlocked, be persuaded to accept the nomination?"

"Show me the deadlock first," replied the Governor of Illinois.

"But if there were a deadlock?"

"I don't believe that's possible. I never thought so and I don't think so now."

"Would you hazard a guess, sir, as to who you think might win it?"

"No, but I think it will be somebody whose name is not Stevenson."

Being a serious presidential contender is a complex operation. Each candidate must field his own task force, for no man without a large organization could possibly be in enough places and do all the things necessary to get the nomination. Behind every serious candidate can always be found several trusted strategists—sometimes colorfully called "kingmakers."

Franklin Roosevelt's nomination in 1932 was

made possible in large part by the efforts of two men, Louis McHenry Howe and James Farley. Two decades before Roosevelt became president, Louis Howe dreamed that one day F.D.R. would make the White House. When Roosevelt was stricken with polio in 1921, it was Howe who insisted that this would not permanently keep young Franklin out of politics. All during Roosevelt's discouraging siege of illness, Howe wrote letters across the country over the future candidate's signature. And he never permitted Roosevelt to be photographed unless he was in a cheerful mood.

Jim Farley, the other "kingmaker," spent two years before the 1932 convention campaigning for Roosevelt's nomination. In those days before extensive commercial air transportion, Farley logged 32,-000 miles. His position as Exalted Ruler of the Elks gave him an excuse to tour the country soliciting votes without attracting undue attention. Thousands of politicians received letters signed "Jim" in green ink. It was reputed, moreover, that Farley could meet half a dozen people in Painted Post, New Mexico, and years later remember whether their wives had asthma or sinus trouble. Looking back over this campaign, Farley wrote: "National politics is big business, and we set about the task of mastering every detail that would have a bearing on the nomination of a Presidential candidate. In the end this mastery of detail was a primary cause in bringing about the nomination of our candidate at Chicago."

Another legendary kingmaker is Marcus Alonzo Hanna. Mark Hanna, a Cleveland industrialist, first met William McKinley in 1878 when McKinley was defending strikers against Hanna's company. So impressed was Hanna that a few years later he retired from business to devote himself to making McKinley the president of the United States. It took Hanna 14 years to put McKinley across. And by the time of the 1896 convention, as one authority put it, the two men "were so closely bound together that they merged into a single personality."

Not all would-be kingmakers, of course, are as sure-footed or as successful as Farley and Hanna. One noted New York politician, Thurlow Weed, confided in a letter written in 1858 that to install William Seward in the White House was "a purpose which for 20 years [has] engrossed my thoughts and controlled my action." But at the 1860 Republican convention, Weed was outmaneuvered and his candidate overtaken by Abraham Lincoln.

In at least two cases the kingmakers have been presidents. The extent to which a chief executive can make his influence felt is illustrated by John Garner's remark that without a president's support no candidacy is better than "a can of stale beer." President Andrew Jackson picked Martin Van Buren as his successor in 1836. And in 1908 President Theodore

Roosevelt determined that he would be succeeded by William Howard Taft. "Terrible Teddy" is said to have jestingly laid down the law: "Take Taft or you'll get me." But Woodrow Wilson felt quite differently: "It is intolerable," he wrote in 1916, "that any President should be permitted to determine who should succeed him, himself, or another."

So far no mention has been made of where presidential nominees come from. What are their backgrounds, occupations, professions?

Twenty-nine men have been elected president of the United States; 11 of them have been military heroes. In fact, every American war except World War I and Korea has produced at least one president.

Since our convention system started in 1832, there have been 17 elections in which military heroes have been nominees. Three times both parties nominated a former military man in the same year. Of the 14 elections in which a military hero opposed a civilian, the ex-soldier won nine times.

From its first presidential candidate to its most recent, the Republican party has been more inclined to choose military heroes than the Democrats. At the "maiden" GOP convention in 1856, the party picked John Frémont, a regular army officer whose exploratory probes had won him the name "Pathfinder of the Rockies." The Civil War provided the Republicans with four Union generals for

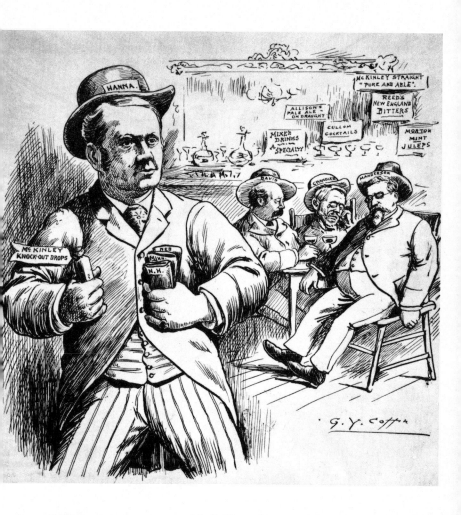

THAT DEADLY DOPE—*Mark Hanna's successful pre-convention strategy in 1896, on McKinley's behalf, is pictured as "doping" the other candidate managers.*

Elections Since 1832 in Which Military Heroes
Were Nominated

Year	Military Heroes	vs.	Civilians
1832	*Jackson		Clay
1836	W. H. Harrison		*Van Buren
1840	*W. H. Harrison		Van Buren
1848	*Taylor		
	Cass		
1852	*Pierce		
	Scott		
1856	Frémont		*Buchanan
1864	McClellan		*Lincoln
1868	*Grant		Seymour
1872	*Grant		Greeley
1878	*Hayes		Tilden
1880	*Garfield		
	Hancock		
1888	*B. Harrison		Cleveland
1892	B. Harrison		*Cleveland
1904	*T. Roosevelt		Parker
1912	T. Roosevelt		*Wilson
			Taft
1952	*Eisenhower		Stevenson
1956	*Eisenhower		Stevenson

* Elected.

nominees, and all were elected. Teddy Roosevelt, the
"Rough Rider" of the Spanish-American War, used
his army exploits to capture the New York governorship and then went on to the vice-presidency and
the White House. Dwight Eisenhower, of course,
was the most recent military man nominated by the

Republicans. During this same period, the Democrats turned to former soldiers only twice—Civil
War Generals McClellan and Hancock.

For almost a century, governors have been looked
to as top-ranking presidential candidate material. In
the 15 elections since the turn of the century, the
Republicans and Democrats have 16 times given the
nomination to governors. And all three third-party
candidates strong enough to win electoral votes since
1900 were one-time governors—Theodore Roosevelt
(1912), Robert LaFollette (1924), and J. Strom Thur-
mond (1948).

Yet it was not until 1868 that the conventions
gave the presidential nomination to an incumbent
governor. The Democrats' selection of Governor
Horatio Seymour of New York opened a new era in
presidential nominations. In 1876, for the first time
both parties were running governors—Governor
Rutherford Hayes (R., Ohio) vs. Governor Samuel
Tilden (D., New York).

Today, being a governor of a large state almost
automatically makes a man a serious contender for
the presidential nomination. Practically no amount
of protest will persuade the political observers that
a governor of New York does not dream of moving
to the White House. And historically, the pundits
are probably right, as the table on page 39 illustrates.

When the annual governors' conference got un-
derway at Bolton Landing, New York, in 1954, a

In 1848, General Zachary ("Old Rough and Ready") Taylor was nominated by the Whigs. A hostile cartoonist called attention to his military background, but the voters made him the first regular Army man to be president.

small boy asked, "Do all governors want to be presidents?" "No, young man," answered an observer, "Some of them just want to choose him."

New York Governors Who Sought
Presidential Nomination

Governor	Nominated	Denied Nomination	General Election Won	General Election Lost
Van Buren	2	1	1	1
Seward		1		
Seymour	1			1
Tilden	1			1
Cleveland	3		2	1
Hill		1		
*T. Roosevelt	2	1	1	1
Hughes	1			1
Smith	1	3		1
F. D. Roosevelt	4		4	
†Dewey	2			2
†Harriman		1		
12	17	8	8	9

* Includes losing 1912 GOP nomination and losing election on Bull Moose ticket.
† Denied nomination once before being elected Governor.

Even when the Founding Fathers were debating how we should select our chief executive, Elbridge Gerry of Massachusetts actually proposed that the president be appointed by the governors of the several states. But this suggestion found little favor, and Edmond Randolph of Virginia complained that the governors would never support a "strong figure" for the presidency. Randolph was, of course, mistaken. James Madison was another who objected to entrusting governors with such a sacred mission. He thought that great pressures would be brought upon them and that they would be too much "courted and intrigued with by the Candidates, and by their partizans, and by ministers of foreign powers."

Yet today governors are the most influential bloc in selecting the nominee. Effective preconvention work by governors played a large part in securing the nomination of Al Smith in 1928, Roosevelt in 1932, and Landon in 1936. Thomas E. Dewey, then governor of New York, used a 1943 strategy conference of the 26 Republican governors as the springboard for his successful campaign for the presidential nomination in 1944. In 1952, Governors Dewey, Sherman Adams of New Hampshire, and James Duff of Pennsylvania were major forces in the Eisenhower victory. And the drive for the 1960 Democratic nomination of Senator John Kennedy of Massachusetts has been spearheaded by Governor Abraham A. Ribicoff of Connecticut and Ohio's Governor Michael Di Salle.

Every fourth year the question of the relative availability of governors and senators as presidential candidates comes up. The governor starts with an advantage. The presidency, as Lord Bryce remarked, is "but an enlarged copy of the State Governor," and any governor's advocate will argue that his man has the training, background, and experience to be chief executive. The nature of the governor's job also makes him less vulnerable than a senator. For example, a senator in the first session of the 86th Congress probably voted on more than 1,000 bills and resolutions and over 40,000 nominations; each vote may have pleased someone, but it may also have angered many. The governors avoid this occupational hazard. Furthermore, the governor is the political boss of his state; he controls the state patronage and, in all probability, the state delegation to the nominating convention. If he heads a large state delegation, this gives him a very comfortable cushion to rest on. New York, for example, has almost one-sixth of the votes needed to win a nomination, and after 1960 California will hold almost the same strategic position.

Quite apart from the advantages of a governorship, however, there are some signs that a Senate seat is no longer the liability it once was. Television has given the national legislator a new forum. The televised Senate investigation of crime certainly catapulted Estes Kefauver into a front-runner position at the 1952 Democratic convention.

A record crop of potential 1960 Democratic nominees comes from the Senate. Yet they are all relative newcomers to the upper chamber. Lyndon Johnson and Hubert Humphrey were first elected in 1948, John Kennedy and Stuart Symington in 1952. If a senator is to make a serious bid for the presidency, must he do it in his early years? Do men after a long stint of service in the Senate become too closely identified in the public mind with that body?

With few exceptions, the history of legislators as presidential candidates has been an unhappy string of rejections at the polls. Able senators like Henry Clay, Daniel Webster, Stephen Douglas, Arthur Vandenberg, and Robert Taft never received enough popular support to reach the White House. And of the one man in this century to go directly from the Senate to the presidency, the Republican New York *Herald Tribune* commented: "We had hoped that a man of undoubted courage, vision, and executive ability would be chosen [by the 1920 Republican convention], but we have instead Warren Gamaliel Harding."

Occasionally, presidential candidates have been men without outstanding military careers or experience as governors or senators. These could be considered "the exceptions that prove the rule." One such nominee was Alton B. Parker, perhaps the least known of any major-party standard-bearer. The Democratic convention of 1904 picked Parker, the chief judge of the New York Court of Appeals, very likely because his personality and philosophy were the opposite of William Jennings Bryan's, who had lost the presidency in 1896 and 1900.

Horace Greeley, Liberal Republican and Democratic candidate in 1872, was primarily known as a newspaper publisher. William Howard Taft had a long public career as a federal judge, governor of the Philippines, and secretary of war. And Herbert Hoover, elected as a Republican in 1928, was originally a mining engineer. In World War I, he had become widely acclaimed for his European relief work, and at the time of his nomination, he was secretary of commerce.

Another exception, Wendell Willkie, GOP nominee in 1940, violated the political rule that a candidate should not be too closely bound to a special interest. Before his sudden entry into national politics, he had been head of Commonwealth and Southern, a public utilities holding company. Willkie, in defying both the party apparatus and the laws of probability, struck a new vein of political force: the politically interested amateur. By organizing and exerting pressure from outside the party hierarchy he set the pattern for effective action later by such groups as the "Volunteers for Stevenson" and the "Citizens for Eisenhower."

One of our greatest presidents was boosted into prominence by a most unusual event: Lincoln became famous with defeat. National recognition came to him largely through his unsuccessful campaign to unseat Senator Stephen A. Douglas in 1858. Lincoln tells how he was going home after his senatorial loss, brooding silently as he walked through the rainy night. Suddenly he stumbled and clutched out desperately to regain his balance. But then, he said, it came over him that it was just a slip and not a fall. How right he was, for two years later he emerged from the ashes of defeat to become the president of the United States.

☆ ☆ ☆ *Availability: The Thirty Men*

William Howard Taft was fond of saying that in any town of 5,000 he could find an American eminently qualified to sit on the Supreme Court. But what of the presidency? Quite clearly we do recruit our presidents from a natural aristocracy, and some experts feel that as few as 30 belong to it.

Presidential candidates are picked according to rigid rules of availability. Our public opinion sifts potential candidates through a fine sieve that allows to pass only governors from the largest states, some members of Congress, an occasional vice-president or cabinet member, and a handful of famous generals, educators, publishers, and industrialists. Among the rejects are women, men under the age of

35, those not born American citizens, the infirm and the aged, and the members of certain minority groups or religions.

Every factor that might influence a voter is carefully dusted off as the party chieftains weigh the capabilities and qualifications of competing candidates. Even where a man was born, grew up, and now lives is an important consideration to the "slate-makers." It has been a hundred years since a southerner was a major presidential candidate. Why should the parties pick a southerner as long as the South votes overwhelmingly Democratic? A northern Democrat rarely loses a southern state, but a southern presidential candidate might lose northern votes that would otherwise go to his party.

Neither have the Mountain states produced any presidential candidates. Arizona, Colorado, Idaho, Montana, Nevada, New Mexico, Utah, and Wyoming have made notable contributions to national leadership through their representatives in Congress, but these seven states combined have only 28 electoral votes, or just one more than the state of Illinois.

Two factors are responsible for this situation: first, candidates from large states usually have a tidy package of delegates, just from their own state alone, when they enter a convention; second, candidates who have already demonstrated that they can win public elective office in a large state are in a stronger position to convince political leaders that they have what it takes to carry the electoral votes of our large industrial states, such as New York, Pennsylvania, Ohio, Illinois, and California. Not often—only in the victories of Grant (1868), Hayes (1876), and Truman (1948)—does a candidate lose New York and win the presidency. More than merely unpredictable, New York holds 45 out of 537 electoral votes. And considering that the two major candidates were separated by only 37 electoral votes in 1884, by 23 in 1916, and by one in 1876, the pivotal character of the Empire State cannot be underestimated.

If there were "anti-trust" laws governing presidential nominations, New York and the Middle West would surely have been convicted of monopolizing the conventions over the last hundred years. The Democrats and Republicans have nominated 53 men since 1856, and 40 of them have come from either New York or the Middle West.

A candidate who can claim roots in both New York and the Middle West is doubly blessed. Such was the fortune of Wendell Willkie: Indiana-born and a New Yorker when nominated. This combination later inspired Harold Ickes to call him "The Barefoot Boy from Wall Street." Dwight D. Eisenhower was a delegate's dream: being born in Texas, reared in Kansas, and having a voting address in New York, where he was president of Columbia University at the time of his first nomination.

While only 12 states have produced presidential

Presidential Candidates, 1856-1956

New York Candidates	Number of Nominations	Mid-West Candidates	Number of Nominations	Candidates from Other States	Number of Nominations
Seymour	1	Lincoln	2	Buchanan (Pa.)	1
Greeley	1	*Douglas	1	Frémont (Cal.)	1
Tilden	1	Grant	2	*Breckenridge (Ky.)	1
Cleveland	3	Hayes	1	McClellan (N.J.)	1
†T. Roosevelt	1	Garfield	1	Hancock (Pa.)	1
Parker	1	Harrison	2	Blaine (Me.)	1
Hughes	1	McKinley	2	Wilson (N.J.)	2
Smith	1	Bryan	3	Davis (W. Va.)	1
F. D. Roosevelt	4	Taft	2	Hoover (Cal.)	2
Willkie	1	Harding	1	Coolidge (Mass.)	1
Dewey	2	Cox	1	‡Eisenhower (Pa.)	1
‡Eisenhower	1	Landon	1		
		Truman	1		
		Stevenson	2		
	18		22		13

* In 1860, just before the Civil War, the Democrats split and nominated two candidates.
† Also ran as Progressive Party candidate in 1912.
‡ Resided in New York in 1952 and Pennsylvania in 1956.

candidates since 1856, the shape of things to come
may be different. Until now the Pacific states have
produced only two presidential candidates: John C.
Frémont, the first GOP nominee, in 1856, and Herbert Hoover, in 1928. A steady population shift to
California in recent years has greatly enhanced its
political importance. After New York, its 32 electoral votes tie with Pennsylvania's for second place.
Moreover, the 1960 census is expected to give California an additional seven electoral votes, while New
York and Pennsylvania will probably lose three votes
each. By 1965 population experts expect California
to pass New York.

Besides geography, several factors can make one
candidate more "available" than another. Until 1928,
when Al Smith ran for president, the only Catholic
to receive a nomination was Charles O'Conor.
O'Conor was a noted New York lawyer who had
been counsel for Confederate President Jefferson
Davis in his treason trial. But O'Conor ran on a
minor party ticket in 1872 and received fewer than
30,000 votes.

Conjecture seems never-ending about whether a
Catholic can win a presidential election. The 1958
election of three new United States senators and two
governors who were Catholics suggests that some religious prejudice is beginning to recede. In Decem-
ber 1959, the Gallup poll asked, "If your party nominated a generally well-qualified man for President,

and he happened to be a Catholic, would you vote
for him?" The response:

Yes	69%
No	20%
Don't Know	11%

Age is also a consideration in judging a candidate's
ability to win a nomination and election. In 1952,
Vice-President Alben Barkley's biggest liability in
his quest for the Democratic presidential nomination
lay in his advancing years. He was nearly 75 at the
time. Most presidential candidates have been in their
early fifties. But the range is wide: the youngest candidate for president was the "boy orator of the
Platte," William Jennings Bryan, who was only 36
when he stormed the Democratic convention of 1896
with the "Cross of Gold" speech; the oldest candidate
was William Henry Harrison, who was 68. James
Buchanan was 65 when he ran in 1856, and the Republicans tried to use this against him by nickname-
ing the Pennsylvanian "Old Fogey."

Buchanan's nomination was singular for another
reason: he was the only president to remain a bach-
elor. His opponents even tried to make his bachelor-
hood an issue with the campaign doggerel, "Whoever
heard in all his life / Of a candidate without a wife?"
Apparently it had little effect on the voters, for he
won the election.

Another delicate personal matter that sometimes

creeps into presidential nominating politics is whether a potential candidate has been divorced. A poll taken by Elmo Roper in 1952 demonstrated that only 3% of the people felt that divorce would make any difference in their vote, suggesting that this issue seems to be a less important one than it was once thought to be in American politics.

Sometimes the route to a presidential nomination is to run as a "favorite son." A favorite son is often a senator or governor. While it is true that as a tribute for past services a state will place its favorite son in nomination, give him a floor demonstration and vote for him on at least one ballot, there is a more important motivation behind favorite-son candidacies: the favorite son is part of a well-worked-out strategy (1) to hold the delegation together, (2) to put the state in the best bargaining position, and (3) to wait until a serious contender gains the upper hand and then climb aboard the bandwagon.

It's a cardinal rule in politics, as the late Senator Claude Swanson once said, "never to wait till the train leaves the station before climbing aboard." Thus when the Democratic members of Florida's congressional delegation unanimously voted to endorse Senator George Smathers as a favorite-son candidate, their spokesman frankly stated that the move was designed to improve the state's bargaining position at the 1960 convention. When a favorite son enters a presidential primary in his own state, he is generally given a free ride; out-of-state candidates usually steer clear. Senator William Knowland, a man who once had presidential aspirations, summed it up accurately when he said: "It is always a dangerous maneuver to enter a state where there is a favorite-son candidate. . . . Ordinarily one avoids a contest in a candidate's home state, . . . partly out of courtesy and partly out of risk of defeat." For this reason, as a strategy to slow down the front-runner, lagging candidates try to promote favorite-son candidacies in states that hold primaries.

In a sense, every presidential candidate is a favorite son. Grover Cleveland in 1892 and Franklin Roosevelt in 1932 are the only nominees who won without a majority of their own state delegation behind them.

The most romanticized entry in the presidential nominating sweepstakes is the "dark horse." Normally he emerges out of a deadlock between two serious contenders. He is strictly an American phenomenon, rising out of our fluid system of leadership succession and our peculiar genius for compromise. The dark horse is unknown in the parliamentary democracies in which leadership is the natural end product of years of party service. But under our system, conventions suddenly unite behind an obscure candidate. Moreover, such compromise choices frequently go on to win in November; six of the ten men who can be considered dark horses were elected.

First of the dark horses was James K. Polk, speaker of the House of Representatives, who emerged the winner on the ninth ballot at the Democratic convention of 1844. The deadlock that made Polk's victory possible was between ex-President Martin Van Buren and Senator Lewis Cass of Michigan. Through seven fruitless ballots Polk's name was never mentioned. On the eighth he received 44 votes out of 266. But on the ninth, largely through the efforts of historian George Bancroft, he received all 266 votes. To play up his anonymity during the canvass, the opposition kept hooting, "Who is James K. Polk?"

In 1852, the Democrats again chose a dark horse— and one even less known than Polk. On the forty-ninth ballot they nominated Franklin Pierce, a former New Hampshire senator who had been out of politics for ten years. When a group of friends informed him of his selection, Pierce gasped, "My God, gentlemen, you could not have told a more astonished man!" During the campaign, the Democrats tried to parlay their two dark horses with the slogan, "We Polked you in 1844 and we shall Pierce you in 1852."

Later, in 1868, after casting 21 ballots without making a nomination, the Democrats turned to Horatio Seymour. In many ways Seymour was not a dark horse, because as governor of New York he was eminently available. Yet, oddly enough, he was little known outside his state and was almost violent in his opposition to making the race. Refusing to allow his name to be placed in nomination, he received no votes until the twenty-second ballot when, having left the convention hall, he was unanimously made the choice of the gathering.

The Republicans too have had many a potential party split healed by a candidate from "left field." When the 1876 convention was hopelessly divided between the forces of James G. Blaine and the Liberal Republicans, the party turned to a dark horse, Rutherford B. Hayes, on the seventh ballot. Four years later the GOP chose a man who not only was opposed to making the race, but was actually the campaign manager of an avowed candidate. James A. Garfield jumped to his feet to protest that he was not a candidate, but Chairman George Hoar promptly ruled him out of order. The convention then proceeded to nominate Garfield on the thirty-sixth ballot, and later Hoar commented, "I do not believe it ever happened before that anybody who attempted to decline the Presidency of the United States was to be prevented by a point of order."

Bryan's first of three nominations, the one in 1896, was unusual in the annals of dark-horse nominations because it was not the result of a deadlock. Bryan literally rose on the wings of words. At 36 his only political qualification was two terms as congress-

THE MODERN JOSHUA—*The walls of the 1896 Demo-cratic convention in Chicago came tumbling down when William Jennings Bryan delivered his "Cross of Gold" speech.*

man from Nebraska. It would have been highly presumptuous for the "boy orator" to have opened a preconvention headquarters or announced his candidacy. In any case, the nomination appeared to be sewed up for "Silver Dick" Bland, a veteran congressman from Missouri. Yet Bryan labored through most of the night before he was to give his now famous speech, working over his old material, and picking out the most effective phrases in his repertoire. Years later a young page boy who was in the convention hall, named Harry Truman, recalled that Bryan's "bell-like" voice reached out to the 17,000 people in the audience. With a flowing, ecclesiastical rhetoric, he electrified the convention with a speech that ended: "You shall not press down upon the brows of labor this crown of thorns, you shall not crucify mankind upon a cross of gold." This performance "stole" the nomination on the fifth ballot.

The closest the convention system has come to breaking down was in 1924, when the Democrats balloted through nine sweltering July days in Madison Square Garden. This convention placed 16 candidates in nomination, gave 59 men votes for the presidency, and took 103 ballots before reaching agreement. The deadlock was between Governor Alfred E. Smith of New York and William Gibbs McAdoo of California, son-in-law of Woodrow Wilson. Through most of the sessions, the two main contenders each had more than one-third of the votes—

enough to veto the other under the two-thirds rule. Yet, although hopelessly stalemated, McAdoo refused to release his delegates, and Smith protected himself by following suit. Against this stalemate, no dark horse could gain the initial footing to stampede the convention. After five days and 77 ballots, the candidates' managers worked through Sunday trying to end the deadlock. Through Tuesday—and 86 ballots—the proceedings droned. Both McAdoo and Smith had now lost their veto power. Finally, on Wednesday, after the main entries had already torn the convention apart, McAdoo released his delegates. In the press section, H. L. Mencken beat out a new lead on his dispatch to the Baltimore *Sun:* "Everything is uncertain in this convention, but one thing: John W. Davis will never be nominated." The next day the convention quickly agreed on Davis, who had received just 31 votes on the opening ballot. Mencken was stunned for the moment, then snapped, "Why that's incredible! I've already sent off a story that it's impossible. I wonder if those idiots in Baltimore will know enough to strike out the negative?"

Ironically, this record-breaking convention was the first ever to be broadcast. All over the country people were glued to the wireless. Even the staid cabinet meeting of President Coolidge was rudely interrupted by the convention noises. Never again could the political convention be a family affair. Radio brought the nation to the rostrum and onto

AW, GIVE A FELLER A CHANCE!—*The two-thirds rule caused the 103 ballot deadlock at the 1924 Democratic convention. William Gibbs McAdoo failed to get the necessary vote, but blocked other candidates by refusing to release his delegates.*

the convention floor. Perhaps this first experience taught the lesson that if a party overloads the circuits with intense bitterness the electorate may take its votes elsewhere—for the able Davis was overwhelmingly defeated.

The most recent nomination that had some of the features of a dark-horse victory was that of Wendell Willkie in 1940. Willkie did become an active candidate and did wage a whirlwind preconvention campaign, but he was unknown to the delegates and had never run for public office before. The Republican party, in fact, could hardly call him its own, for he had actually been listed as a Democrat in the 1940 edition of *Who's Who in America*. As president of one of the largest public utility systems, he was rarely in the limelight. His fight against Roosevelt's public power policy had been his only appearance in page-one news. Yet he defeated such well known leaders as Arthur Vandenberg, Robert Taft, and Thomas Dewey, winning the GOP nomination on the sixth ballot.

Often too much emphasis is put on the dark horse as one whom fate lifts from oblivion to the high pedestal of presidential nomination. Of course, an element of fate and/or fortuitous political timing is involved in all nominations. But it should be recognized that being a dark horse can be a shrewd strategy well worked out in advance. Perhaps it was a stab in the dark, but six months before the 1920 convention, campaign manager Harry Daugherty correctly predicted the nomination of Dark-Horse Warren Harding on the tenth ballot. And the dark-horse nomination of Willkie was carefully engineered by such able molders of public opinion as Oren Root, the Cowles publishing family, and Russell Davenport, a former editor of *Fortune Magazine.*

Generally a president can have a second nomination if he wants it. But there have been exceptions —the defeat of President Franklin Pierce at the 1856 Democratic convention and the failure of Chester Arthur, who had succeeded on the death of Garfield, to win the nomination in 1884, although he was an active candidate. Yet, by the standards of politics, which can change from day to day, renomination of the incumbent is one of the ground rules. After all, a party in power must stand or fall on its record— which is the president's record. It would be a tactical error to rebuff a president who will have to be defended at least until November.

A defeated candidate's chance of getting another nomination is dependent in some degree on how badly he lost and in what circumstances. Men like Alton B. Parker, James Cox, and Alfred Landon were so trounced in 1904, 1920, and 1936 that they were never again thought of as contenders. But the dynamic William Jennings Bryan was able to get his party's nomination three times (1896, 1900, 1908), even though he was never elected. In 1912, his swing

Two incumbent Roosevelt presidents had an easy time rounding up delegates. "The Cowboy President," Theodore Roosevelt, won the 1904 Republican nomination on the first ballot. His Democratic cousin, Franklin D. Roosevelt, handily captured the third nomination in 1940, although challenged by his vice president, "Cactus Jack" Garner of Texas.

to Wilson very likely was a critical factor in bringing about Wilson's nomination. And as late as 1924, Bryan was a powerful enough influence to get his brother the vice-presidential nomination. With some justification, in his later years Bryan remarked, "I seem to rule the nation by losing elections."

Grover Cleveland won a renomination after suffering defeat for re-election—and went on to win. In 1948, Dewey became the only Republican loser of a presidential election to be given a second chance. Most recently, of course, Adlai Stevenson, the Democratic nominee in 1952, won an easy first-ballot nomination in 1956. Are the prospects for "recommissioning" defeated presidential candidates looking better? Recent history suggests the possibility.

☆ ☆ ☆ *Political Housekeeper:*
The National Committee

On a typical November day, eight months before the 1960 conventions, and before anyone had formally tossed his hat into the ring, five undeclared presidential candidates were in orbit. Governor Nelson Rockefeller of New York landed in Los Angeles and within 14 hours held a press conference, made two speeches, granted three television interviews, and had four conferences with Republican leaders. On the same day, in Long Beach, California, Senator Stuart Symington of Missouri was photographed sampling biscuits before talking to the National Grange convention. Senator Hubert Humphrey of Minnesota had spoken to the Grange the day before. Across the country, the Vice-President, Richard Nixon of California arrived in central Wisconsin, called a press conference, delivered a speech, and stopped off at the local Elks Club. In Marshfield, Wisconsin, 31 miles away, Senator John Kennedy of Massachusetts met with 1,200 Democrats, then moved on to Milwaukee for the state party convention. Senator Humphrey was scheduled to address the convention the next day.

While the candidates criss-cross the country at a furious pace, the hard hand-in-glove work of tuning up the nominating machinery moves slowly along. In Washington the national committees of both parties are busy organizing the coming presidential conventions. Ever since the first national committee was set up by the Democratic convention of 1848, they have had the responsibility for convening the conventions, making the temporary rolls, and performing the many housekeeping chores necessary to bring the delegates together every four years.

Initially the national committee consisted of a man from every state and territory, but in 1920 membership was broadened to include an equal number of committeewomen. Moreover, since 1952 the Republicans have given committee representation to the state chairmen from every state that went Republican in the last presidential election, or that has a majority of Republicans in its congressional delegation or a Republican governor.

National committees nominally elect their chairmen, but actually the choice is made by the president or the presidential nominee. Democratic Chairman Paul Butler is a rare exception: in 1954 he became the first man since 1912 to be chosen by the committee itself rather than by a White House occupant or aspirant.

What else distinguishes the man who is the most important organizer of the nominating convention? Occasionally the national chairman is simultaneously an elected official, like Republican Senator Thurston Morton of Kentucky. Seldom, however, is the post a stepping stone to public office. In former years, the national chairman frequently doubled as postmaster general in the president's cabinet. But the office has now become a full-time job with a salary if the chairman chooses to receive compensation.

Since 1928, the national chairman of the Democratic party has always been a Catholic. The only Jewish chairman was Victor Rosewater, who headed the Republican national committee in 1912.

The first official act setting the nominating process in motion is the issuance of the call by the national chairman. This ordinarily takes place in March of the convention year and is in the form of a letter to all county chairmen notifying them of the date of the convention and the number of delegates to which each state is entitled.

The chairman also divides his committee into working groups to handle all the convention arrangements—housing, program planning, press relations, concessions, tickets, and transportation. Additionally, he chooses and supervises the committees that will draw up the convention rules, pick the convention officials, and hold initial hearings on delegate seating contests.

Selection of the temporary chairman and the other temporary convention officers is also the function of the national committee. The convention usually goes along with the committee. But things didn't go according to form at the 1884 Republican convention. Backers of James G. Blaine, in control of the national committee, had their candidate for temporary chairman vetoed in a heated floor fight. The convention instead chose John Lynch, a former Mississippi slave, and the only Negro to ever serve as presiding officer of a major party convention.

A major decision before the national committee is where to hold the convention. When the Democrats go to Los Angeles in 1960, it will be the first time that city has played host to a nominating convention and only the third time that a convention has been held on the West Coast. The Democrats in 1920 and the Republicans in 1956 met in San Francisco. Both 1956 and 1960 California conventions are interpreted as recognition of the new political power of the Pacific states.

The national committee calls for bids from all cities interested in becoming the site of the convention. Then it weighs such factors as auditorium seating capacity, space available for news media, convention-hall facilities for caucuses, number of hotel rooms, parking and transportation, and the amount the city will contribute to defray committee expenses.

The subcommittee that investigates proposed sites is nowadays ever mindful that a national convention attracts over 1,500 newspaper and magazine reporters, some 2,500 radio and television workers, between 2,500 and 4,500 delegates and alternates, and possibly as many as 45,000 spectators.

Adequate housing has always been a major convention headache. Way back in 1884, a cartoon depicted convention delegates sleeping in bureau drawers and was captioned, Room Clerk to Delegate, "You may have the lower drawer, sir." But it was no joke when a reporter found 132 people using billiard tables for beds at an early Chicago convention. And at the 1936 GOP convention, held in Cleveland, there was such an acute room shortage that some delegates were bedded on steamers in Lake Erie.

Finding the right convention hall poses equally difficult problems. Chicago built the Wigwam in less than six weeks to house the 1860 Republican convention. It cost a modest five or six thousand dollars, but two thousand remained unpaid at convention time. The Chicago *Tribune* urged the local populace to contribute chairs for gallery use, and a 25¢ ad-

Republican National Chairman Thomas H. Carter calls for bids for the 1896 convention.

There has always been keen competition among cities to become the site of the presidential conventions.

mission fee was finally resorted to in order to retire the debt. A newly finished hall in Minneapolis, which housed the 1892 GOP convention, kept dropping gummy resin from the unseasoned pine in the ceiling onto the heads of the delegates below.

In 1960, Los Angeles won out over Philadelphia, Chicago, New York, San Francisco, and Miami Beach with a cash offer of $350,000, a guarantee of 12,000 hotel rooms, and the use of a new $5,000,000 arena on the edge of the downtown business area, which will have a main floor the size of a football field and a seating capacity of 17,000.

Of course, simple politics also affects the choice of a convention city. Before the Civil War, Baltimore was the favorite meeting ground of the Democratic party. Every party conclave between 1832 and 1852 was held there. It was a good choice because it was as far north as the slave-state delegates wished to venture and as far south as the northerners would go.

Discrimination against Negro delegates frequently enters any discussion of possible convention cities. In fact, in over a hundred years the major parties have held only one convention below the Mason-Dixie line; that was the 1928 Democratic convention in Houston.

Many potential candidates try to influence the choice of a site. For example, Norman Judd, who nominated Lincoln in 1860, scored a great coup by getting the national committee to pick Chicago, in

Lincoln's home state. Then Judd, a railroad attorney, insured that his candidate would have a favorable reception by getting his clients to carry Lincoln supporters to Chicago free of charge. And to be doubly sure that the galleries would be packed, hundreds of fake admission tickets to the convention hall were printed and distributed to Lincoln men.

Al Smith also outmaneuvered his rivals by persuading the Democratic national committee to hold the 1924 convention in New York City. And by holding the Democratic convention of 1952 in Chicago, pro-Stevenson forces were able to impress the delegates with the Illinois governor's oratorical prowess before the balloting began.

Franklin Roosevelt too liked to have the Democratic national convention meet in Chicago. Three of his four presidential nominations took place in the Windy City. The reason for his preference, according to Jim Farley, was that Chicago's Mayor Kelly could be counted on to take care of such details as filling the stands with partisans, installing a loudspeaker system with a Roosevelt bias and a leather-lunged city commissioner in the convention-hall basement to lead the cheering.

For its central location, as well as an occasional political reason, Chicago is the overwhelming favorite as the convention site. It is the most equitable spot for westward and eastward traveling delegations to meet, and when the Republicans meet there in

1960 it will be the city's twenty-third national convention.

Before 1932 it was rare to find both conventions in the same city. However, the two parties teamed up on a site in 1932, 1944, 1948, and 1952. While they have gone separate ways since, there is still pressure from the television networks to hold the conventions at the same place so as to avoid duplicating the expense of setting up and moving the elaborate equipment necessary to provide full coverage.

A far knottier problem for the national committee than room space or auditorium size is apportionment. In determining how many votes each delegation should have, the Republicans use a basic formula giving each state twice the number of its congressional delegation. A state therefore is entitled to two delegates from each congressional district plus four at large (reflecting the two United States Senate seats).

In addition to a basic representation, the parties have awarded bonus votes. Both parties' systems of rewarding the faithful resulted from problems created by the "Solid South."

In the post-reconstruction period, the southern states swung overwhelmingly to the Democratic party. Yet the Republican convention continued to recognize the South on a par with other sections of the country, so that states making no contribution to Republican presidential victories still retained a strong voice in convention decisions. This gross mal-apportionment led to a serious rupture at the 1912 convention. The galleries chanted in unison—"Railroad tactics!" and "Choo, choo, choo"—as the solid southern delegations helped "steam-roll" the convention for William Howard Taft. And the power of these "rotten boroughs" led to a reform that gave states added delegates for delivering the vote in November.

At the 1960 Republican convention, a state will be allowed six extra delegates if it went for President Eisenhower in 1956 or for a Republican senator or governor since then. Congressional districts which cast at least 2,000 votes for Mr. Eisenhower or for the party's nominee for Congress in 1958 will get one vote, and those districts giving more than 10,000 votes to these candidates will be entitled to an additional delegate.

The problem of the one-party South, of course, reversed the problem for the Democrats. Until 1936 the South had a veto power over presidential candidates, because it was a party rule that a nomination had to be carried by a two-thirds vote. But when the rule was abolished in favor of a majority vote, the Democratic South was compensated with a bonus system.

In 1959, however, the Democratic National Committee scrapped its bonus system, and now each state gets two and a half votes for each of its United States senators and representatives. Thus Kansas, which has six representatives and two senators, gets 20 votes. Alabama gets 28 votes for its nine representatives and two senators, rather than $27\frac{1}{2}$, because when the distribution results in a fractional vote the next highest number is used. Another new feature of this apportionment plan gives each member of the national committee a half vote in the convention. Since each state has a committeeman and a committee-woman, this will add one vote to every delegation's total. There is one more complication: to get approval for this new method of apportionment Chairman Butler had to promise that no state would have fewer votes than it had in 1956. Therefore, a state like Arizona, with a four man congressional delegation, would ordinarily be entitled to 10 votes. But because it had 16 votes in the 1956 convention, it will get 17 votes in 1960 (*i.e.,* its 1956 vote of 16 plus one additional vote for its national committee members).

Oddly enough, adding up the number of votes does not determine the size of the convention. The Democratic party has long permitted delegates to cast less than one vote. This "fractional voting" is not allowed by the Republicans. The theory of the fractional vote is that it brings more people into the convention and sometimes heals a local fight, because by increasing the number of delegates, two rival groups in a state may both be given representation.

Sometimes, however, the Democrats have found fractional voting getting out of hand as they did in 1940, when one Mississippi district, entitled to two votes, sent 54 delegates to cast them. The rule has now been changed to allow no delegate to cast less than one-half vote.

All convention bodies are doubled in size, of course, because each delegate has an alternate. The stand-by has no vote, but must be ready to fill in should his delegate be unable to attend a convention session. Like the understudy waiting in the wings, the alternate occasionally finds himself in the spotlight. This happened to one gentleman at the 1952 Democratic convention. While the nation listened, having waited for months to hear whom President Truman favored, the Chairman recognized a man in the Missouri delegation:

> Mr. Chairman, my name is Gavin and I am the alternate for the President of the United States. I have said a number of times that the President's choice was my choice and so I shall quote, not read, a request from the President:
>> "I hope you will see your way clear to cast a vote for Adlai Stevenson for the nomination. Signed, Harry Truman."

Among the national committee's many functions, one is held in abeyance that could become extremely important. It is authorized to fill vacancies on the ticket. Twice this has happened. In 1860, Benjamin

Fitzpatrick of Alabama declined the Democratic vice-presidential nomination and was replaced, and in 1912 Republican vice-presidential candidate James Sherman died before the election.

Most of the administrative functions of the national committees—the intensive preparations that must precede the opening of the conventions—are handled by the committees' professional staffs, which work out of large suites located in downtown Washington office buildings. For these men and women, working out the details of convention management is just another duty in the vineyard of American politics—soon to be followed by general election campaigns, mid-term congressional elections, day-to-day charges and countercharges, and, in four quick years, another national convention.

☆ ☆ ☆ *Corralling the Delegates*

Edward J. Flynn, political boss of Bronx County, New York, and a delegate to the Democratic national convention in 1932, knew that a majority of his constituents favored Al Smith for the presidential nomination. Yet he voted for Franklin Roosevelt. Why did he knowingly reject the sentiment of his district's voters? Because, said Flynn, he felt that Roosevelt was the better qualified and could win. Flynn was following the Burkian philosophy that a representative is chosen to vote his own conscience as to what is best for his people, party, and country.

Yet, today, the trend in preconvention campaigning is toward greater reliance on public-opinion polls. More and more the candidate directs his appeal to the general public rather than to the party leaders who will be convention delegates. His success is measured by his rating in polls conducted by George Gallup, Elmo Roper, Louis Harris, and others. Armed with bundles of these early temperature readings taken on Main Street or among minority groups, workers, farmers, and professional people, the candidate or his managers then work on the delegates or potential delegates with "See, I can win" or "He can't win."

Polling has run an uneven course in presidential politics. While a post-card survey conducted by *Literary Digest,* based on millions of automobile registrants and telephone subscribers, was proving that Alf Landon would be elected president in 1936, a sampling by Dr. George Gallup forecast a Roosevelt landslide with considerable accuracy.

By 1940 the politicians already had one eye on the polls as they convened to pick presidential nominees. The Republicans watched Wendell Willkie, not even a serious contender from January through April, appear suddenly in Gallup's May findings. By mid-June he had jumped to second place, and by the end of the month the Republican national convention had chosen him to carry its standard.

Although the pollsters were jolted by Truman's victory in 1948, having predicted that Dewey would win, the use of polls still formed the backbone of Eisenhower's strategy in 1952. The popular General eclipsed Robert Taft in all preconvention polls, and his managers forcefully drove home the point that Eisenhower was the only sure winner.

Polling as a campaign tactic reached a record high in 1960. Candidates and their supporters have released a steady flood of polls, not only of the scientific variety, but of county chairmen, former delegates, congressmen, congressmen's constituents, and any other group that might possibly influence the outcome of the convention. This development prompted ex-President Truman to write:

> I have felt for a long time that political polls have injected an unhealthy element into free elections and were being used to some degree to influence political trends. In my own case, long before the 1948 campaign, I knew that the political pollsters could not get at the true state of mind of the electorate. I have observed that many people properly resent the intrusion upon their political privacy by outsiders.
>
> They either refuse to divulge what is really in their minds or purposely mislead their questioners. I would suggest that the current crop of preconventions polls only add to political confusion and constitute a doubtful criteria of how the public will vote a year from now.

Yet, despite Mr. Truman's warning, the importance now attributed to polls is demonstrated by one reporter's estimate that candidates and political par-

ties will pay six million dollars for private surveys in
the 1960 campaigns.

No one is more concerned with these popularity
polls than the candidate managers—the men Jim
Farley called "the political drummers." Who are
these agents who travel from Kennebunk to West
Wenatchee peddling the wares of their candidates?

When the candidate is a United States senator,
the nucleus of his day-to-day campaign organization
is his Washington office staff. Senator Kennedy relies heavily on his youthful legislative assistant, Ted
Sorensen One of Senator Humphrey's advisers is his
administrative assistant, Herbert Waters, a former
California newspaper editor. Vice-President Nixon
delegates many of his campaign functions to three
of the young men on his staff: Bob Finch, the former Los Angeles County Republican chairman;
Charles McWhorter, a New York lawyer; and press
aide Herbert Klein, a San Diego newsman.

The preconvention campaign staff of an aspiring
governor differs slightly. Since he controls the state
party, his managers are often local party officials.
Governor Rockefeller's two chief supporters are New
York Republican Chairman L. Judson Morhouse
and National Committeeman George Hinman. Governor Robert Meyner of New Jersey is generally rep-
resented by Robert Burkhardt, the executive di-
rector of the State Democratic Committee. And
Governor G. Mennen Williams' top lieutenants are

Democratic National Committeeman Thomas Quimby and Michigan State Chairman Neil Staebler, an Ann Arbor businessman.

Nor does it hurt a candidate to have a tightly knit family to help carry his banner. In this respect few clans can rival the attractive Kennedys. When John first ran for the Senate in 1952, his mother and sisters organized "kaffee klatsches" all over Massachusetts. They were immensely popular campaigners and may again start "pouring for Jack." Add the Senator's lovely wife, Jackie, and you have a powerful vote-getting formula. The male side of the family is equally sure-footed on the campaign trail. Led by millionaire father Joseph P. Kennedy, a former ambassador to Great Britain, the circle includes brother Bob, ex-counsel to the Senate rackets committee, and Ted, who managed his brother to an impressive victory in 1958, as well as brothers-in-law Sargent Shriver, a rising Chicago executive and civic leader, Stephen Smith, and Actor Peter Lawford, who is reported to have said, "Anything I can possibly do, I'll do—although I don't know exactly what it will be just yet. Maybe opening meat markets."

A candidate's "task force" also has some influential volunteers. The Humphrey group includes Jim Rowe and Max Kampelman, both Washington lawyers, and Jim Loeb, who publishes a newspaper in Saranac Lake, New York. Senator Symington leaves many political chores to Louis McGee, a Kansas City insurance man, Lambert O'Malley, a Chicago lawyer, and Missouri Congressman Charles Brown, a 39-year-old television and radio producer specializing in hillbilly programs. Meanwhile, Adlai Stevenson's law partner, William Blair, generally looks out for his interests. And one of the top advisers to Nixon is Leonard Hall, former Republican national committee chairman.

Basically, campaign managers must adapt themselves to two types of situations: states that choose delegates by party convention, and states whose delegates are elected by primary. The 50 states present almost 50 variations on the two basic systems of delegate selection.

The 35 states using the convention method of picking delegates operate roughly in this manner: If you live in Pocahontas County, Iowa, and wish to take part in the selection of state delegates to the national convention of your party, you first attend a precinct caucus. Here your job is to choose delegates to a county convention. This convention in turn selects delegates to a state convention. And finally the state convention picks the "at large" delegates to the national presidential convention.

The convention system of selecting delegates is, so to speak, to hold meetings in the shape of a pyramid, starting first with the smallest political unit:

Order	Level of meetings
1	PRECINCT
2	COUNTY
3	STATE
4	NATIONAL

However, because under the national rules of apportionment some delegates will come from congressional districts, rather than the whole state, the delegates from the counties must also meet with the other counties in their congressional district to choose their share of the national convention delegation. Thus, prior to the state convention, the delegates from Pocahontas County will meet with the delegates from Winnebago, Humboldt, Kossuth, and the rest of the 15 counties that make up Iowa's Sixth Congressional District. Therefore some of the Iowa national delegation will be chosen by a slightly different pyramid:

PRECINCT

COUNTY

CONGRESSIONAL DISTRICT

NATIONAL PRESIDENTIAL CONVENTION

On the other hand, approximately 40% of the convention delegates are chosen by presidential primaries. It is the results of these 15 states and the District of Columbia that will receive most of the public and press notice during the preconvention period. For this reason, the primaries take on political significance out of all proportion to the number of delegates actually picked in this manner.

Because some primaries are outright popularity contests between rivals for the nomination, the rise or fall of potential presidential candidates often rests on the vote for a few delegates in small states using the primary system. In some primaries, candidates for delegate are pledged to a particular presidential aspirant. In six states, however, the presidential preference of the voters is not legally binding on the elected delegates, and in several other states the delegates are obligated to vote for the primary winner on only one, or possibly two, ballots at the national convention.

Because it is the first of the presidential year, the primary election in New Hampshire probably has the greatest psychological import. The state's voters who braved the winds and snow of early March in 1952 and 1956 registered decisive political decisions. In 1952, while General Eisenhower was still an inactive candidate on duty in Europe, New Hampshire Governor Sherman Adams skillfully directed a task force that won a victory over Robert Taft, from which the Taft candidacy never recovered. In 1956, the New Hampshire primary again played a dramatic role in national Republican politics. The "dump

Nixon" campaign was completely undercut when the Vice-President received 22,000 votes even though his name was not on the ballot.

Certainly Senator Kefauver's strong position at the 1952 Democratic convention was a result of his victories in 12 of the 15 state primaries he entered. But his preconvention campaign stalled in 1956, and after defeat in the Florida and California primaries he withdrew in favor of Adlai Stevenson.

Primary defeats also shipwrecked the presidential hopes of Wendell Willkie in 1944 and Harold Stassen in 1948. Internationalist-minded Willkie waged an aggressive campaign in Wisconsin, then considered an isolationist stronghold, and when he failed to win a single delegate he withdrew from the campaign. In the Oregon primary of 1948, Thomas Dewey accepted Stassen's challenge to a debate, won the primary by coming from behind in a theatrical finish, and set Stassen's star in eclipse.

Wisconsin was the first state to provide for direct election of delegates to national conventions (1905), but Oregon introduced the presidential primary (1910). By 1916, this reform, giving voters a more direct voice in the nominating process, had been enacted in half the states. Enthusiasm for the system started to wane by 1936. A revival began in 1948, but now another decline has set in. Two states have repealed their primary laws since 1956.

Among the arguments against the primary is that

NEW HAMPSHIRE
POLITICAL
PEEP SHOW

FIRST GLIMPSE—*The nation awaits the "first glimpse" of the relative strength of the presidential contenders—the New Hampshire primary in March.*

in some states it actually thwarts the will of the party members. This can happen in states using the "open primary" system. Here a voter does not have to be a registered party member to cast a ballot in the party primary. Some observers believe that many Democrats chose to vote for Earl Warren on the Republican ballot in the 1952 Wisconsin primary. And in Minnesota in 1956, when the Republicans did not have a contest in their primary, it seems evident that many switched party lines to vote for Kefauver in an effort to embarrass Stevenson and Senator Hubert Humphrey, whose state organization was actively behind the former Illinois governor.

Professional politicians complain that primaries often give them little freedom of action—if their state law binds them to a candidate, they may lose the initiative to get the best possible deal for the state party at the convention. They further object to the primary system on the grounds that it commits them too long before the convention. They contend that often the rival candidates' positions become known *after* their primary election.

Active presidential contenders complain that the primaries are an almost inhuman strain on their health, forcing them to rush from state to state, waging in each the equivalent of a full-scale gubernatorial race. The rigors of political campaigning have reached such a point that one writer, observing recent contests for the governorship of Florida, comments, "Since 1936, two of Florida's governors became gray-headed during the campaign and the first months of office, three were seriously ill while in office, and one died of a heart ailment, generally believed to have been caused by the strain of his election campaign." Kefauver, recalling his 1952 primary experiences, said, "There were days when I just didn't think I could last out until Chicago." And in the first phase of the 1960 presidential campaign alone, Senator John Kennedy traveled more than 100,000 miles, toured 20 states, and reportedly ate 173 lunches and dinners of creamed chicken and green peas.

Primaries create two other worries for the candidate: Time and Money. For the candidates who hold public office, especially governors, the grueling primaries mean weeks away from their pressing duties at home. When Nelson Rockefeller withdrew from the 1960 race for the GOP presidential nomination, he gave as his main reason: "Any quest of the nomination would entail a massive struggle—in primary elections throughout the nation, demanding so greatly of my time and energy that it would make impossible the fulfillment of my obligations as Governor of New York." Furthermore, while it may not have been a factor in Rockefeller's decision, it takes a great deal of cash to set up organizations in each state that holds a primary. It is impossible to uncover exactly how much a preconvention campaign

ESTES

ADLAI

PRIMARY STATES

Hy Rosen

JOUSTING RIVALS-

costs, because there is no law requiring reports of contributions and expenditures. When a Senate committee investigated the 1920 preconvention expenses, it found that nearly three million dollars had been spent on behalf of all the candidates. One advertising agency estimated that Dewey and Stassen spent $100,000 each just in the 1948 Oregon primary, a figure that may confirm Will Rogers' observation that politics has "got so expensive that it takes a lot of money even to get beat with." Dean Alexander Heard of the University of North Carolina estimates that preconvention efforts on behalf of General Eisenhower in 1952 totalled at least $2.5 million; while the Taft campaign was even more expensive. He also figures that the total Stevenson outlay before the 1956 Democratic convention ran to at least $1.5 million, "plus other hundreds of thousands of dollars in gifts of goods and services."

What this means is that the "wait-and-see" candidates may be forced to declare their intention earlier. For until a candidacy is out in the open it is extremely difficult to raise funds. In this respect, it is noteworthy that Senator Eugene McCarthy and Governor Orville Freeman of Minnesota set up a "Humphrey for President Committee" on July 15, 1959—presumably one year to the day before the 1960 Democratic national convention would start balloting for president.

Another complaint lodged against the primary

system is that it is costly to the state. Iowa held a presidential primary in 1916 in which only one candidate from each party was on the ballot. That vote cost the state $200,000, and the next year it quickly repealed the law. The presidential primary does avoid, however, the high cost of litigation that often stems from the selection of delegates by the convention system. Since 1912, no delegation elected in a primary has been involved in a major seating contest.

One of the most objectionable features of the primary, of course, is that it rarely gives the voter a clear choice between the major candidates. The serious contender, knowing the consequences of a primary defeat, will carefully avoid facing a rival in a doubtful state. For this reason the operation of the new Oregon primary system will be carefully watched. Under the 1959 law the secretary of state may put any name on the ballot if the "candidate's candidacy is generally advocated or recognized in national news media throughout the United States." The candidate can get his name removed from the ballot only by "stating without qualification that he is not now and does not intend to become a candidate."

In the final reckoning, the successful candidate will be the most masterful broken-field runner, the one who breaks away from the pack and adroitly weaves through the primaries and state conventions. In all probability, he will be the one with the smoothest functioning staff, the stoutest stamina, and sufficient funds. But he will also have to have something else—that elusive quality called "charisma" by the social scientists and "it" by movie producers. Alistair Cooke, in 1956, described a potential candidate as having "a fairground smile painted on a cardboard cut-out." That contender may have had everything else, but he didn't have "it."

☆ ☆ ☆ *Routine and Reaction:*
Convention Committees at Work

"Will the delegates please take their seats? The convention will be in order." With these words and the steady swat of a gavel the national committee chairman opens a presidential convention. Months of attending to details and arrangements are over; often, years of sparring and planning by the candidates and their managers are about to bear fruit or wither on the vine.

The high mission of a presidential convention is, of course, to select a candidate. But many important tasks remain before the convention swings into an executive mood to select the party standard bearer. Most of this fundamental work is performed in the four full committees of the convention: credentials or contests, rules, permanent organization, and platform or resolutions.

The work of these committees explains why the opening days of a convention are filled with an effervescent display of campaign oratory. The delegates are marking time until the committees report.

Meanwhile, each committee is holding hearings and writing reports under the leadership of a chairman who has long before been selected by the national committee. Traditionally, these committees have been made up of a representative from each delegation, with the exception of the platform committee which has consisted of a man and a woman from each state. In 1960, however, the Democratic national committee adopted a new rule expanding the membership of all four major committees to a male and female delegate from each state.

First to report is the credentials committee. This body acts as a kind of court to determine which delegates are entitled to be seated. In the great majority of cases there are no conflicts. But occasionally some states send two competing delegations to a convention. At the Republican national convention of 1952, there were nearly a hundred delegates involved in seating contests. Republican contests usually generate among the southern delegations. Every South Carolina and Mississippi Republican delegation from 1916 to 1948 was involved in a seating contest. Often these fights are the reflection of a power struggle between two state factions. And they're serious business to the contestants—to the victor may go the control of federal patronage in the state for the next four years.

On a broader canvas, these fights are often between delegations pledged to rival presidential candidates and are closely watched for any early portent of competing candidates' power. In famous Republican conventions, 40 years apart, two statesmen named Taft figured prominently in credential fights.

At the 1912 convention—"The Steamroller Convention"—the credentials committee rejected every claim favoring Theodore Roosevelt and seated every supporter of William Howard Taft. As William Allen White recalled it:

> Slowly, motion by motion, phase by phase, the steamroller crushed its way toward the nomination of Taft. And here is a funny American expression: In the midst of all the rancor and wormwood pumping in the hearts of the delegates, every time a motion was offered by the Taft people, a thousand toots and imitation whistles of the steamroller engine pierced the air sharply, to be greeted with laughter that swept the galleries. An American crowd will have a terrible time behind barricades, or surging up Pennsylvania Avenue to overwhelm the White House. It will probably laugh itself to death on the way.

The galleries may have been amused, but the Roosevelt forces were not. Out they stormed, soon to bolt the party.

In 1952, Taft's son Robert also controlled the credentials committee, which reported favorably on his delegations from Georgia, Louisiana, and Texas. But the Eisenhower strategists carried the fight to the convention floor and, under the banner of "Fair Play," ably marshalled public opinion and uncommitted delegations to pave the way for a first-ballot nomination.

Rules committees often routinely readopt the rules of the last convention, but again, acrimonious set-tos can take place. Franklin Roosevelt's managers wanted to rescind the two-thirds rule at the Democratic convention of 1932. This rule gave the southern bloc a virtual veto over nominations, and it soon became apparent that F.D.R. would lose his southern support if he tampered with this hundred-year-old tradition. Four years later, however, when the President was in complete control of the convention, he successfully pressed for the abolition of the two-thirds rule. Other prominent rules fights have occurred over the unit rule at the Democratic convention of 1884, the loyalty oath at the Republican convention of 1880 and the Democratic convention of 1952, and the rule governing the voting rights of contested delegates at the Republican convention of 1952.

Much of the work of the resolutions committee on the party platform—called "fusions of ambiguity" by Wendell Willkie—has been done long before the convention convenes. Yet a considerable amount of convention time is taken up with this work. First the committee listens patiently to all who have suggestions, a process which at the 1948 Democratic convention was bitingly reported by H. L. Mencken:

> The only active ganglion in the Democratic nervous system was the Committee on Resolutions in session since Wednesday on the theory that it is drawing up the party platform. That theory, of course, is buncombe. . . . But the committee spent the day going through the motions of listening to advocates of a long string of proposed planks. Advocates consisted of representatives from almost innumerable cells of uplift ranging from the Mothers of America to the National Authority for the Ladies Handbag Industry and from the American League for an Undivided Ireland to the United States Committee for United Nations Genocide Convention.

That convention, of course, was drafting an "in-party" platform, since the Democrats controlled the White House. And so Mencken was probably right, for at least since 1928 the president's party has its platform largely designed by the desires of the chief executive. In 1932, when President Hoover was running for reelection, his secretary of the treasury de-

THE QUADRENNIAL PICNIC.

"Mother Democratic Party" greets a proposal to abolish the two-thirds rule in 1932. But it was not until 1936 that the rule was changed.

livered the entire Republican platform (except for one plank) to the waiting convention committee in Chicago.

Cynics are often overly inclined to call all platforms "buncombe." They ignore the fact that a platform issue sometimes explodes on the convention floor with tremendous muzzle velocity. This happened in both parties over the same issue in 1896—the question of unlimited coinage of silver. At the Republican convention, Senator Henry Teller of Colorado wept for the cause of free silver and lost. Then he led his followers out of the party, while the remaining delegates stood on their chairs shouting, "Go, go" and singing "The Battle Hymn of the Republic." But the table was turned at the Democratic convention. The party's historian tells us that the free-silver supporters outdid themselves with oratorical allusions to Washington, Jefferson, Madison, Monroe, Jackson, Lincoln, Cincinnatus, Tiberius, Gracchus, Cato, Cicero, Catiline, Leonidas, Ivanhoe, Henry of Navarre, Peter the Hermit, Cromwell, Danton, Murat, Robespierre, Napoleon, Wellington, Lodi, Austerlitz, Waterloo, Yorktown, and Thermopylae. When the smoke had cleared, an unknown free-silver advocate, William Jennings Bryan, had carried the day for his cause and his candidacy.

Bryan figured in another bitter battle on the floor of Madison Square Garden in 1924. The question was whether to mention the Ku Klux Klan in a plank on religious tolerance. The now aging Nebraskan told the assemblage that after an all-night session of the resolutions committee he had got down on his knees to pray for guidance. Violence threatened to erupt, and the New York police lined the convention hall. An organist blundered into a rendition of "Marching Through Georgia," and the insulted southerners nearly rioted. Finally, the naming of the Klan was defeated by a vote of $542\frac{3}{20}$ to $541\frac{3}{20}$ and the convention proceeded to other business.

The shadow of "John Barleycorn" hovered over both parties' conventions through the 1920's and into the early '30's. In 1928, the Democratic platform finally came out for repeal of the prohibition amendment. But the Republicans stoutly refused to abandon the "noble experiment," even after Senator Wadsworth eloquently pleaded with the resolutions committeemen to vote as they drank.

In recent years, the Democrats have had more floor fights on platform issues than the Republicans. While the GOP has not had such a hassle since 1932, there were two heated roll calls on civil rights proposals at the 1948 Democratic convention.

The fourth of the convention committees—permanent organization—is charged with selecting the permanent chairman. Actually, the national committee recommends a candidate for this key position, and it is rare that its choice is rejected.

THAT PERPLEXING PARAMOUNT PLANK!

*President Herbert Hoover and a nervous Republican ele-
phant look down upon convention leaders wrestling with a
prohibition plank in 1932. In the end the convention refused
to come out for repeal.*

This last happened at the 1932 Democratic convention. Al Smith, the titular head of the party, dominated the national committee and managed to get the committee to endorse his candidate for permanent chairman, Jouett Shouse. However, the forces of Franklin Roosevelt had enough strength to upset the decision on the convention floor and install Senator Tom Walsh of Montana as the presiding officer.

This struggle highlights an important qualification for a permanent chairman. He should not have presidential aspirations. Ideally, the permanent chairman should also maintain an attitude of neutrality toward all active candidates. For, as Thomas O'Neill, the astute observer of the Baltimore *Sun*, tells us:

Great power is implicit in the discretion vested the chairman of a national convention, where few ever know what is happening. He can accept or ignore motions, can order a recess between ballots that will give a hard-pressed faction an opportunity to re-group and rally weakening delegates. Senator Paul Douglas has observed that insiders who control the convention machinery can within limits rig developments for or against a candidate by such dodges as turning off the loudspeakers when an unfavored side is trying to present its case. Recognition can be extended or withheld to those trying to get the floor, and a chairman with a blind side can shut out those whose motions he would squelch.

The advent of the television camera into the convention hall seems to have increased the importance of the nontelevised committees; the parties have attempted to reduce the dullness of the convention sessions by shifting more of the routine work to the committees. The convention committees provide an effective means of accomplishing much of the convention's basic work away from the glare of klieg lights. Yet while committee action is often quietly and quickly approved, it always has a sensitive fuse that can at any moment ignite a bitter fight on the convention floor.

CAN HE DO IT?

CIVIL RIGHTS PLANK

SOUTH

NORTH

CHICAGO

Hy Rosen

The writing of a civil rights plank at a Democratic National Convention is a delicate task and there is always the possibility of a bitter floor fight.

☆ ☆ ☆ *Who Are the Delegates?*

Walt Whitman, one of the most eloquent exponents of American democracy, looked over a typical presidential nominating convention of the pre-Civil War era and despaired that "the members who composed it were" (among worse things): conspirators, murderers, kept editors, spaniels well trained to carry and fetch, terrorists, slave-catchers, mail-riflers, spies, bribers, spongers, carriers of concealed weapons, and the born freedom-sellers of the earth.

Yet when a study sponsored by the Brookings Institution surveyed a recent convention, it found: "The delegates of 1952 were better educated, less boss-ridden, more adjusted to the requirements of an open political system and generally more trustworthy in all respects than those of a half century earlier."

Of the many factors tending to raise the caliber of convention delegates over the past hundred years, some of the most important are the integration of immigrant groups, the virtual disappearance of state-wide political bosses, rising standards of education, more vigorous enforcement of high standards in the awarding of government contracts, Civil Service and the Hatch Act, inclusion of women as delegates, growing alertness of civic and other interested groups, party apportionment reforms, and the increased significance of the presidential primaries.

The first woman stepped onto the convention floor relatively recently, but she still predated the women's suffrage amendment. In 1892, two ladies from Wyoming were seated as alternate delegates. In that year, Mrs. J. Ellen Foster of Iowa also became the first woman to address a Republican convention. Rising, she prophetically said, "We are here to help you—and we have come to stay." A woman was seated as a full delegate by 1900. And the 1956 Democratic convention had 287 women delegates and 391 alternates, while the Republicans honored 208 women as delegates and 355 as alternate delegates.

What's the average convention delegate like? Studies by Daniel Tuttle, Jr., Charles Braucher, and a Brookings Institution task force draw this composite picture of a delegate: in his early fifties, Protestant, attended college, earning slightly more than $10,000 a year, a lawyer, possibly a party official, and probably a "repeater" (having served as a delegate before). This, of course, is only a composite, and all interests and groups are represented to varying degrees.

The diversity of the delegates can be glimpsed from these percentages of delegates to the 1948 conventions:

Religion	*Democrats*	*Republicans*
Catholic	27.5%	6.1%
Jewish	6.1	.7
Education		
Post-graduate training	34.3	34.0
Only elementary school	5.3	3.2
Income per year		
Over $50,000	4.0	9.4
Under $3,500	9.3	6.3
Occupation		
Business	23.4	25.8
Farming	6.6	7.5

Negroes have often been members of southern delegations at Republican conventions since the Civil War. At the 1952 GOP gathering, there were at least 82 Negro delegates and alternates; the Democrats had an estimated 43 Negroes serving on delegations that year.

Labor union members are delegates, too. In 1948, 9.7% of the Democratic delegates and 2.7% of the Republicans belonged to a union. Certain state party organizations, in fact, allot seats to organized labor. Both the CIO and AFL were given a place in the 1948 Connecticut delegation to the Democratic convention; Kentucky made room for a member of the United Mine Workers; and Arkansas gave a partial vote to one of the railway brotherhoods.

Serving as a delegate can be an expensive proposition. Some states expect a contribution to the party in return for the privilege of being a delegate. In 1952, the Republican party of Indiana required delegates to pay $500 in advance of their selection; would-be Democratic delegates in the state were assessed $200. On the other hand, North Dakota law provides for a payment of $200 to the delegates for their convention expenses, and in Wisconsin the Republican organization offers $100 to delegates to help defray their costs. However, most delegates pay their own way. A delegate's personal expenses, of course, vary with the distance he lives from the convention site. When both conventions were held in Chicago in 1952, the average expense for a delegate ran between $200 and $500. But to come all the way from Hawaii probably cost a delegate a minimum of $700.

For many delegates this is the most fascinating experience of their lives, an event to tell and retell to the neighbors back home and to the grandchildren for years to come. From the moment a man is selected as a convention delegate an aura of surprise, color, and excitement enters his everyday world. For some Democratic delegates, there is the opportunity to hobnob with the greats at Perle Mesta's lavish party—an institution established in 1948. For most, the 1960 Democratic convention in Los Angeles will also mean seeing Disneyland during adjournments—an event enticingly dangled by Chairman Paul Butler to insure that the convention runs on schedule.

When New Hampshireman J. Duane Squires, who had never run for political office before, was elected delegate to the 1952 Republican convention, he had no idea of the avalanche of mail that was about to descend upon him. Later, in amazement, he wrote:

> For many days in June I received an average of 40 letters in each mail delivery. These came from all over the country; from pressure groups asking endorsement of their platform proposals; from sponsors of the various candidates for the Presidential nomination urging each one of us to back his candidate; from assorted crackpots of all persuasions . . . and from the candidates themselves. For example, Candidate Taft mailed each delegate a handsomely framed autographed photograph of himself, to say nothing of a "Bob Taft" necktie. Special groups in Chicago sent shopping cards for use in certain of the big stores; courtesy cards for the horse race track in that city; invitations to night clubs, famed eating establishments, and sporting goods stores. I made an endeavor to organize and file my mail and it fills today a cardboard carton two feet in length.

On reaching the convention city the delegate steps into an atmosphere of absolute frenzy. The old grad is swept back to his wildest days on the campus; the reserved farmer has a wide sombrero planted on his dome by a lovely convention belle; the quiet banker parades with a campaign button as big as a fried egg on his narrow lapel; the man in the gray flannel suit tipples with the man in high boots and shoestring tie; and anyone is apt to share a taxi with Chief Spotted Crow. How does one spot this South Dakota Indian? Simple, as the delegates in 1948 found out. He's the one in full regalia who never takes a bus, because, as he put it, "Ugh, bus ruffle feathers."

☆ ☆ ☆ *Seventy-five Million Words*

"Plainly on furlough from some home for extinct volcanoes" was Mencken's estimation of convention orators. The output is staggering. In 1956 the flow of words to the convention floor was estimated by one statistician at 75 million, or enough to fill 1,000 novels.

First of the major addresses, once called by Mark Sullivan a combination of "oratory, grand opera, and hog-calling," is the "Keynote," traditionally given by the temporary chairman. The keynoter's job is to carbonate party spirits and whip up enthusiasm among the waiting delegates. Sometimes the speaker accomplishes this mission. Clare Booth Luce in 1944 delivered a memorable pep talk to her fellow Re-

publicans in which she coined the term "G. I. Joe."
Other keynoters are often less successful. Viewers of
the 1952 conventions will recall that General Douglas MacArthur's address to the Republicans probably damaged his political standing. And some felt
that Governor Paul Dever of Massachusetts, the
Democratic keynoter, was defeated for re-election
that November as a result of his unimpressive appearance at the convention.

The parties' elder statesmen always make an appearance. Herbert Hoover has addressed every Republican convention since 1932, and Harry Truman
will undoubtedly become a tradition at Democratic
conventions.

With television cameras zeroed in on the rostrum,
now is the time to give candidates for state office
some free publicity. Mayor Hubert Humphrey of
Minneapolis, running for the Senate in 1948, urged
his party "to get out of the shadows of states rights
and into the bright sunshine of human rights." Several southern delegations bolted the convention, but
Humphrey won his election. The Republicans too
parade their office-seekers before the convention and
in 1956 thirteen senatorial candidates made speeches.

"Ladies Day" at the conventions has also become
an institution. A gay bonnet and a pretty face add a
dash of color to the three days before the nominations begin. In 1956, seven Democratic congress-
women and 13 Republican ladies delivered short

talks on topics ranging from "Civil Service" to "New Ideas."

Finally, the committees report.

First is the credentials committee. This report at the 1952 Republican convention threw the hall into an uproar. Fighting over the contested delegation from Georgia, Senator Everett Dirksen pointed his finger at Thomas Dewey:

> "I tried to be one of his best campaigners, and you ask him whether or not I didn't go into 18 states one year and 23 states the next. Re-examine your heart before you take this action in support of the minority report, because *we followed you before and you took us down the path to defeat.*"

> (Deafening applause and boos.)

> TV announcer: "Mr. Dirksen is advocating the seating of the Taft delegation. There's a great deal of confusion out there. There goes a fight. There's a photographer getting in trouble. I don't know who is hitting whom. Somebody got knocked down, but it's pretty hard to tell who it was. The officers were in the middle of it—they really are having a time here tonight."

> Senator Dirksen continues: "This is no place for Republicans to be booing any other Republican. (Applause) Fellow delegates, I assure you that I didn't mean to precipitate a controversy. . . ."

A bumper crop of fights over the convention rules also developed in 1952. At the outset of the Republican convention, Governor Arthur Langlie of Washington introduced a resolution to keep contested delegates from voting until their contests were resolved. These delegates favored Senator Taft, and a bitter floor fight resulted between the forces of the rival candidates. The Eisenhower camp won the rules change, a psychologically important first victory.

The heated rules fight among the Democrats was a bitter carry-over from the 1948 election. Michigan's Senator Blair Moody proposed that every state delegation pledge that the convention nominees would appear on their state ballot in November. This so-called "Loyalty Oath" was designed to prevent another Dixiecrat-type bolt. After bitter debate, the Moody resolution passed in a session that finally recessed at 2:05 A.M.

The Democrats returned to this subject in 1956 when they adopted a new rule to remove any national committeeman who, in the event of a bolt, fails to support the national ticket actively. In 1960, the Democratic national committee will again ask the convention to approve this resolution.

The next report, on permanent organization, rarely causes a stir. Republican Congressman Joseph W. Martin of Massachusetts has served as permanent chairman five times (1940 through 1956), an all-time record. Two Democrats have served as permanent chairman three times, Joseph T. Robinson and Sam

Rayburn, who stepped down in 1960 so he could "see one convention from the floor."

The final committee report usually amounts to a monotonous reading of party planks. In 1956, the Democratic delegates listened to a platform of 15,-000 words (about 30 times the length of the party's first platform in 1840). The intoning of the platform is generally followed by a quick voice-vote. But when there is a fight, it can really rock the rafters. The strong civil-rights stand of the 1948 Democratic convention was too much for the Alabama delegation; the unhappy delegation chairman arose to make an announcement:

> Alabama chairman: "(We) will proceed to walk out of this Convention and return to Alabama . . ."

> (Many boos)

> Chairman: "Has the delegate from Alabama completed his statement?"

> Alabama chairman: "No, the confusion prevented me. . . . Mr. Chairman, I'm also authorized by the Chairman of the State of Mississippi to say to you at this time in this Convention, that in the face of the platform adopted, the delegation from Mississippi could not be true to the people of that great State if they did not join in this walk-out and therefore they join with us, and we bid you good bye."

Some contend the platform should be taken up after the nominations to allow the candidates a greater voice in its formulation. Yet the platform is so general that the nominees can interpret it almost as they see fit. Rarely is there a serious platform-candidate split such as the Democrats presented in 1864, when they adopted a plank calling for an immediate halt to the Civil War and then turned around and nominated Union Army General George McClellan.

With the committee reports disposed of, convention tempo picks up. From now on, events move briskly.

To the next speakers go the honor of nominating candidates for the presidency. Today we are accustomed to a florid flow of nominating oratory, overly ornate and usually too long. Yet this was not always so. In 1860 the name of Lincoln was placed in nomination with 27 words. Norman Judd simply stated:

> I desire on behalf of the delegation from Illinois, to put in nomination as a candidate for the President of the United States, Abraham Lincoln of Illinois.

Supporters of Lincoln's chief rival, William H. Seward, may have felt the Illinois delegation was being overly gabby: the New Yorker was nominated with only 26 words.

In tracing the evolution of the nominating speech, we see that when General Logan nominated Ulysses

Grant eight years later, the speech was still brief. But note the language:

> In the name of the loyal citizens, soldiers and sailors of this great Republic of the United States of America, in the name of liberty, humanity and justice, in the name of the national union of the Republican Party, I nominate Ulysses S. Grant.

By 1880, nominating speeches had taken on a few more ornamental flourishes. Said the blind orator Judge West of James G. Blaine:

> Nominate him and the campfires and beacon lights will illuminate the continent from the Golden Gate to Cleopatra's Needle.

To the true convention *aficionado,* a really memorable nominating speech eases the pain of hours of platitudes. One of the most famous concluded:

> To stand upon the ramparts and die for our principles is heroic. To sally forth to battle and win for our principles is something more than heroic. We offer one who has the will to win, who not only deserves success, but commands it. Victory is his habit: The Happy Warrior, Alfred E. Smith.

That, of course, was the way Franklin D. Roosevelt nominated his candidate at the 1928 Democratic convention.

The nominating speech is followed by seconding

speeches. These are shorter, but more numerous. The record, probably never to be surpassed, was set at the Democratic convention of 1936, when Franklin Roosevelt was seconded 56 times.

Nothing is hit or miss in choosing the nominating and seconding speakers. They are picked to show a candidate's broad appeal. Five men and three women seconded President Eisenhower in 1956. They were: (1) a western dirt farmer, (2) an eastern labor union member, (3) a Texas housewife, (4) a Negro history professor, (5) a southern steel manufacturer, (6) a former Notre Dame football coach, (7) a woman leader in local philanthropy from New England, and (8) the Governor of Maryland.

These key speakers can be picked for other reasons—such as to show party unity. During the 1956 preconvention campaign, Harold Stassen started a "dump Nixon movement," hoping to replace the Vice-President with Governor Christian Herter of Massachusetts. The move fizzled, and, not by accident, Nixon was nominated by Herter and seconded by Stassen at the convention.

Hopefully we are returning to a simpler form of nominating speech. While they retain the embellishments, the parties have at least limited their length, as well as the number of seconding speeches.

Wild demonstrations are carefully scheduled to follow the speeches. Delegates and "ringers" pack the aisles—chanting, singing, shouting, whistling. Do

When Harold Stassen's move to "dump Nixon" failed in 1956, the former Minnesota Governor seconded the Nixon nomination.

they influence the convention outcome? Probably not, for the delegates know they are synthetic and are easily whipped up with amplifiers and organs. Yet they are still an essential ingredient that helps create the heady enthusiasm we all enjoy as we look forward to the climax of the convention—the presidential balloting.

☆ ☆ ☆ *Nominating "The Next*
President of the United States"

Once the clerk of the convention is instructed to call
the roll of the states, the delegates become quiet and
serious. At last the balloting for president begins.

In early conventions, the roll-call order was based
partly on geographical location and partly on the
order in which states entered the Union. However,
at the 1868 Republican convention, controversy
arose over whether Kansas should be called before
West Virginia. Shortly thereafter both parties
changed to an alphabetical system.

"Alabama," calls the clerk.

The Alabama delegation chairman rises to an-
nounce the state's vote.

The chairman always casts the entire vote of his

delegation, a custom dating back to the first Democratic convention. The delegation chairman is usually the state's highest ranking public official. If the party controls the state house, the chairman will probably be the governor. In the absence of a governor, the chairman may be the senior senator or, if the party holds no high office, the state party chairman.

Now the chairman gives the vote and sits down, but it was once proper for each chairman to deliver a short speech in praise of his state and his candidate. When Montana was called at the 1868 Republican convention, the state chairman declaimed, "The mountains of Montana, from whence flow the waters of the Columbia and the Mississippi, are vocal with the name of Grant, to whom she gives two votes!"

In convention voting, the Democratic party has long recognized the "unit rule," under which the state's *entire* vote is recorded the way a *majority* of the delegation votes. At the 1960 Democratic convention, Connecticut Governor Ribicoff has a majority of the delegation pledged to Senator Kennedy. The state's junior senator, Thomas Dodd, favors Lyndon Johnson. Yet, because the state uses the unit rule, Dodd's vote will be recorded for Kennedy. Twenty delegations were bound by this rule in 1952. A major floor fight in 1884 revolved around the unit rule. New York's Tammany Hall tried to rescind the unit rule to get its minority vote counted against

Grover Cleveland. The rule was upheld; Cleveland got the whole vote of the delegation and won the nomination.

States coming early in the voting order are faced with a special question: to commit themselves before the band wagon or not to commit. To avoid this, a delegation can pass and be called again at the end of the roll call.

Any delegate can challenge the vote as reported by the delegation chairman. The delegation is then polled. Calling for the vote of each member of the delegation is very time-consuming. In fact, that is sometimes the reason that it is done—simply as a stalling device to give a delegation added time to work out a trade. Polls, too, allow a delegate to make his position known, or force his hand by compelling him to go on record. Frequently the demand to poll a delegation is a legitimate questioning of the chairman's count. But with television turning each delegate into an actor, polls can be a grand way to show off for the people back home. Concerned lest the long boring polls detract from the show, the Democratic convention of 1956 adopted a new rule under which the convention chairman may send a representative to the delegation to conduct the poll while the rest of the convention proceeds with the roll call.

With tension mounting at the 1952 Republican convention, Marcelino Romani, a delegate from

Puerto Rico, tripping lightly over syntax and logic, requested a poll of his tiny delegation:

Delegate Romani: "I request that the name of the alternate be polled."

TV announcer: "Looks as if we're going to have more trouble polling three Puerto Ricans than they did 90-odd New Yorkers. Apparently the name of the alternate is a tough one, from the way that the secretary looks."

Convention Chairman: "Sergeant at Arms will please clear the aisle. Delegates please be seated, so that we may complete this roll call."

Mr. Romani: "Mr. Chairman, I wish to state that the only alternate here is Mr. Salgado."

Convention Chairman: "The secretary will read the name of the alternate for the delegate from Puerto Rico."

Secretary: "Mrs. Providencia Ramos de Villamil."

Mr. Romani: "What the name please?"

Convention Chairman: "The secretary will be permitted to read the name of the alternate again."

Mr. Romani: "Eet's all right. She not here."

(Loud demonstration)

Long after the heat of the Taft-Eisenhower fight had died down, delegates remembered the laugh provided by Romani.

While the convention votes, the candidate managers are under heavy strain. The scene becomes a supermarket for rumors of last minute "deals." Most famous, perhaps, of the manager's deals occurred at the 1860 Republican convention. Lincoln's manager, David Davis, was desperately trying to get the large Pennsylvania vote, but the delegation was controlled by an industrialist who wanted a cabinet post in return for his support. In the midst of the negotiations, Davis received a telegram from Lincoln: "MAKE NO BARGAINS FOR ME." "Hell!" snapped Davis, "We are here and he is not!" Lincoln received the votes and the Pennsylvanian got his cabinet post.

Franklin Roosevelt was just shy of going over the top on the third ballot in 1932. The Texas delegation, with enough votes to cinch the nomination, was pledged to "Cactus Jack" Garner. Roosevelt's floor manager, Arthur Mullen, claims that he and Texas Senator Tom Connally negotiated the Roosevelt-Garner ticket at a hot dog stand "on wobbly stools, with no one but a sleepy, uninterested, dirty-aproned cook for audience." Connally's reaction was, "We can iron out the details during the day. And will you pass the mustard?" Others say the deal was made between Jim Farley and Sam Rayburn.

The managers swing into operation their carefully made plans. Farley in 1932 laid the groundwork for that moment when the favorite sons drop out by lining up "second choice" support for F.D.R. Harry

Daugherty, master mind of the miraculous Harding nomination in 1920, lent votes to Frank Lowden on the early ballots on the time-tested theory that a candidate must grow in strength; one who starts strong and then slips will rarely recover. Dewey's brain trust in 1948 simulated a bandwagon by announcing the support of a few more states each day, up to the time of the convention balloting. Willkie's staff meticulously compiled a list of the delegates' friends and business associates, which they used to create a last minute barrage of wires and calls from the folks back home.

On the convention floor, the delegations hurriedly caucus. Caucuses go on throughout the convention, and the average delegation usually meets daily in its hotel to keep abreast of developments and plan strategy. Once the balloting begins, a wavering delegation will seek some cranny close by in order to make last-minute plans.

Frequently, conventions get into prolonged deadlocks, such as the one that developed at the 1912 Democratic convention. The New York delegation swung to Champ Clark of Missouri on the tenth ballot—giving him a clear majority. But a two-thirds vote was then necessary to get the Democratic nomination; the balloting continued. By the forty-third ballot, Governor Woodrow Wilson of New Jersey had a majority. Finally on the forty-sixth ballot, he won the nomination. Only once before, in 1844, had a candidate received a majority and still lost the nomination.

Rescinding the two-thirds rule in 1936 lessened the likelihood of such prolonged deadlocks. This is a good thing, says one political writer, who assumes that if the two-thirds rule were still in effect it might be impossible to nominate a candidate because air-conditioning now makes the convention hall so comfortable that the delegates are no longer compelled to compromise on a choice in order to return to the cool comforts of their homes.

It is likely, however, that the television camera more than offsets the air-conditioner as a mechanism to end deadlock. Party leaders are well aware that bad feeling and caustic words inevitable in long floor fights may give the voter-viewer an adverse impression. Political strategists feel there is just too much at stake to slug it out before a watching electorate.

It also takes fewer ballots to reach agreement now because much of the real struggle for the nomination goes on during the preconvention period. As the scene of battle shifts, the convention outcome is becoming more of a foregone conclusion.

However, if a floor fight does develop, the jockeying among the vying factions presents a rare view of the politicians shorn of their protective covers. A common trick of those opposing the front-running candidate is to try to force a recess. The hope is that a night's rest or just a few hours away from the convention hall will cool off the developing enthusiasm. A recess can also be used to give the candidates time to negotiate.

The most dramatic recess occurred at the Republican convention of 1876. The scene was Exposition Hall in Cincinnati, described by one observer as "an ambitious and disappointing railroad depot." James G. Blaine had just received a rousing nomination, in which he was transformed into a "plumed knight." Pandemonium developed; it looked as if Blaine would win a quick nomination. Suddenly the gas lights failed. The convention recessed. The next day the enthusiasm for Blaine had subsided, and the nomination went to Rutherford B. Hayes. History doesn't reveal whether the recess, so devastating to Blaine, was caused by act of God or the hand of a rival candidate's manager.

Recesses also irreparably damaged the chances of two other candidates. Lewis Cass in 1844 and Henry Wallace a hundred years later let the delegates go home for the night while they were ahead, only to return the next day to see the prizes go to James Polk and Harry Truman respectively.

As it becomes clear that one candidate is gaining momentum, other contenders may gang up against the leader. This often makes "strange bedfellows" as opposing sides are thrown together under the pressure of stopping the front-runner. During the fight over the 1956 Democratic vice-presidential nomination, several groups tried to unite behind Senator Kennedy in a vain effort to stop the Kefauver nomination. Such an attempt, of course, involves what politicians call a "deliverable vote"—a very rare commodity. As Senator Taft pointed out in analyzing his 1952 loss: "At one point in the convention it was suggested that I retire and turn over my delegates to General MacArthur or some other candidate. . . . [T]hese delegates were built up as Taft delegates, and I had no power to transfer many of them to anybody."

On the convention floor, the bobbling state standards give the clue that the convention is close to agreement. For a delegation chairman waves his state sign to gain recognition—and possibly change his vote. It happened this way at the Republican convention in 1952:

> TV announcer: "Eisenhower lacks only 10 votes of winning on the first ballot, but he did not win it. And so at the end of the first ballot, Eisenhower had 595 and Taft has an exact 500. This is dreadfully close—very close indeed, especially on the first ballot.
>
> (The Chairman recognizes Senator Thye of Minnesota.)
>
> TV announcer: "This might be very important. Listen carefully."

Senator Thye: "Mr. Chairman, Minnesota wishes to change its [28] vote to Eisenhower!"

(Loud applause and demonstration.)

The dramatic moment when a candidate gets the nomination is sometimes symbolized by a statement from his rival. At the 1952 Democratic convention, the chairman recognized the governor of Tennessee for this announcement:

> Governor Browning: "Mr. Chairman, I rise to suggest a change in the vote of Tennessee, and in doing so I request that Senator Kefauver be permitted to make a brief statement. . . ."
>
> (Cheers)
>
> TV announcer: "This is a big moment for Senator Kefauver if he is allowed to make his statement. There he is. This is Senator Estes Kefauver, who is witnessing on the eve of his birthday the end of his hopes as a presidential candidate for this year at least."
>
> Senator Kefauver: "Mr. Chairman and ladies and gentlemen of the Convention—I am here to express my very deep appreciation to the delegates who have voted for me and who have fought so hard for me here in this convention. . . ."

Thus Estes Kefauver withdrew from the contest, and Adlai Stevenson won the nomination on the third ballot.

As the great political reporter Murat Halstead once wrote, "The storm breaks. That which was to be, is." There is a great rush to change votes. Unless there is a great deal of bitterness, all delegations will support the winner. "Getting on the band wagon" is especially important for states in which the party is in the minority, as the Republicans are in the South. There, the party organization is denied local patronage and has to be extra careful to be in the good graces of the presidential nominee, who may become its only source of political jobs.

The only chores still remaining are the selection of a vice-presidential nominee, acceptance speeches, and passage of routine "resolutions of appreciation."

Standard practice, through most of convention history, was to appoint a "committee to notify the candidate." Some weeks after the convention this group made a pilgrimage to the party standard-bearer's home to surprise him with the stale news of his selection. However, this quaint custom was shattered when Franklin D. Roosevelt flew to Chicago in 1932 to accept his nomination personally. In a memorable speech, he coined the name by which his four-term administration was to be known to history: "I pledge you, I pledge myself, to a *new deal* for the American people."

Inaugurating the acceptance speech as the presidential campaign kickoff, Roosevelt again, at the 1936 convention, roused his partisans by stating,

"This generation of Americans has a rendezvous with destiny."

A presidential nominee's acceptance speech was also the occasion for an important announcement in 1948. Harry S. Truman used the Democratic convention rostrum to rally the troops, springing this surprise: "On the twenty-sixth day of July, which out in Missouri they call Turnip Day, I'm going to call that [Republican] Congress back. . . ."

The delegates have now made their choice. They roar approval and are impatient now to get on with it—to select a vice-presidential nominee—and then hurry home.

☆ ☆ ☆ *The Running Mate*

"My country," wrote our first vice-president, John Adams, "has contrived for me the most insignificant office that ever the invention of man contrived or his imagination conceived." This opinion has been restated, generally less eloquently, many times since 1793.

The limited constitutional and historical role of the American vice-president has had an important bearing on the final work of the national convention—the selection of a running mate.

Yet the "Throttlebottom" appraisal of the vice-presidency has changed considerably since 1953. Under President Eisenhower much real responsibility has been given to the vice-president; greatly increasing the possibility of veeps' becoming leading contenders for the presidential nomination. With this new importance, we may well see greater vigor in fights for the vice-presidential nomination. Clearly, this was a factor in the exciting battle between Kefauver and Kennedy at the 1956 Democratic convention.

If it happens in the future that losing contenders for the presidential nomination seek the vice-presidency, it will bear some resemblance to our original constitutional system. For, through the election of 1800, the vice-president was the man who received the second highest number of votes for the presidency. The Constitution at first made no distinction between electoral balloting for the two offices. But a deadlock in the electoral college in 1800, when Thomas Jefferson and Aaron Burr received an equal number of votes, threw the election into the House of Representatives. Jefferson's election in this manner led to the 12th Amendment to the Constitution.

Because the nation was undergoing a hardening of party lines, the likelihood of more ties was evident. With the rise of political parties, the presidential electors would no longer vote on the highly independent basis envisioned by the Founding Fathers. Rather than put the personal qualifications of the candidates first, they would now vote according to party lines. So the Constitution was changed to require electors to vote separately for a presidential and a vice-presidential candidate.

The vice-president is now nominated in the hurried closing hours of the convention. The delegates generally act out a weak carbon copy of the presidential nominating script—speeches of nomination, seconding, demonstrations, balloting and roll calls.

Many considerations lie behind the choice of a presidential running mate. Sometimes even the sound of a name is factored into the contest. After Alfred Landon received the Republican presidential nomination in 1936, some wag suggested that if Governor Styles Bridges of New Hampshire was put on the ticket, the Democrats would laugh their way to victory with the slogan "Landon Bridge's falling down." That year Frank Knox won the nomination, and the Grand Old Party marched into the campaign with the battle cry "Off the Rocks with Landon and Knox."

A much more serious consideration for the slate-makers is geography. One of our stubbornly persistent traditions is the idea of "balancing the ticket." Rarely have both presidential and vice-presidential nominees been from the same section of the country. Notable exceptions to this basic rule have been the winning Republican ticket of 1868, U.S. Grant (Illinois) and Schuyler Colfax (Indiana); the 1936 Republican slate of Landon (Kansas) and Knox (Illinois); and the two times that Nebraskan William Jennings Bryan ran with fellow midwesterners— Adlai Stevenson of Illinois in 1900 (grandfather of the Democratic nominee in 1952 and 1956) and John Kern of Indiana in 1908.

Throughout our history the odds have told us that if a presidential candidate came from New York, his running mate would probably be a midwesterner. If the top of the ticket was from a central state, the process was reversed. Typically, the Democrats took their presidential candidates from New York and then gave the second spot to a native of the Middle West. But the Democratic convention reversed this order in 1920, with James Cox of Ohio as the standard bearer and a young man from New York as the vice-presidential nominee—Franklin D. Roosevelt. Later this New Yorker helped select vice-presidents from the Midwest: Henry Wallace of Iowa in 1940 and Harry Truman of Missouri in 1944.

The consistency of this pattern emerges from most Democratic slates of the last half of the nineteenth century:

Democratic Tickets

Year	For President	For Vice-President
1868	Horatio Seymour NEW YORK	Francis Blair MISSOURI
1872	Horace Greely NEW YORK	B. Gratz Brown MISSOURI

1876	Samuel Tilden NEW YORK	Thomas Hendricks INDIANA
1884	Grover Cleveland NEW YORK	Thomas Hendricks INDIANA
1888	Grover Cleveland NEW YORK	Allen Thurman OHIO
1892	Grover Cleveland NEW YORK	Adlai Stevenson ILLINOIS

On several occasions, Republicans have used the same formula. Teddy Roosevelt in 1904 and Charles Evans Hughes in 1916—both New Yorkers—ran with Charles Fairbanks of Indiana. Usually, however, the Republican practice has been to reverse the Democratic order and nominate midwesterners for the top position and New Yorkers for vice-president.

Republican Tickets

Year	For President	For Vice-President
1876	Rutherford Hayes OHIO	William Wheeler NEW YORK
1880	James Garfield OHIO	Chester Arthur NEW YORK
1888	Benjamin Harrison INDIANA	Levi Morton NEW YORK
1892	Benjamin Harrison INDIANA	Whitelaw Reid NEW YORK
1900	William McKinley OHIO	Theodore Roosevelt NEW YORK
1908 } 1912 }	William Howard Taft OHIO	James Sherman NEW YORK

Geography is still a highly important consideration for the ticket-makers, but today there are different emphases. The new tendency in the Democratic
party is to balance the slate "vertically" rather than
"horizontally." Instead of choosing an easterner and
a midwesterner, the party usually picks a *northerner*
for president and a *southerner* for vice-president.
This formula produced a New York-Texas ticket of
F.D.R. and "Cactus Jack" Garner in 1932 and 1936;
Al Smith from "the sidewalks of New York" running
with Joe Robinson of Arkansas in 1928; and Adlai
Stevenson from Illinois coupled with southern Senators John Sparkman of Alabama (1952) and Estes
Kefauver of Tennessee (1956).

The Republican party changed its geographic
priorities to try to cash in on the emerging political
power of the Far West. In 1928 and 1932, its presidential nominee was Herbert Hoover of California.
And in the 1940's and '50's, the GOP usually picked
its vice-presidential candidate from the Pacific states:
Senator Charles McNary of Oregon in 1940, California Governor Earl Warren in 1948, Senator Richard Nixon of California four years later and again
in 1956.

A re-examination of this emphasis on geographic
balance may be needed, for of the last 12 vice-presidential candidates, five lost their home state in the
general election. They were, Kefauver (1956), War-

ren (1948), Wallace and McNary (1940), and Knox (1936).

McNary's name suggests another consideration in choosing the running mate. The Oregonian ran with Wendell Willkie, a leading advocate of private power. But McNary was an acknowledged supporter of public power. His nomination was not just a geographic balance to Willkie, but an ideological balance as well. And when the prohibition issue threatened the harmony of the 1928 Democratic convention, the party attempted to compose its policy difference by forming an Al Smith-Joe Robinson ticket, which prompted one writer to say that the Democratic donkey left its Houston site "with a *wet* head and wagging a *dry* tail."

So it is that whether or not candidates for the nation's two highest elective offices have the same policy orientation is not necessarily a factor in the selection process. Sometimes the candidates don't even know each other. This was true of the Cox-Roosevelt ticket in 1920, as well as of the Willkie-McNary slate in 1940.

Age is not important in choosing vice-presidential candidates. Never has there been a strong feeling about picking younger men in order to groom them for eventual succession. Although, like the presidential nominee, the average vice-presidential candidate has been in his early fifties, there has been a wider age range. Youngest vice-presidential candidate was

An important consideration in choosing the 1940 Republican slate was that vice presidential candidate McNary was from the West Coast and presidential candidate Willkie was from the East Coast.

John Breckenridge, only 35 when he won office in 1856. Richard Nixon was 39 when first elected in 1952. At the other extreme, the Democrats put up an 81-year-old man for vice-president in 1904. The ancient candidate was Henry G. Davis of West Virginia, a millionaire mine-owner, railroad magnate, and banker. Hopefully, the party expected him to underwrite the campaign. But the old fellow didn't jump at the bait and refused to make a sizable contribution to the war-chest.

The presidential tradition that an incumbent is assured of renomination if he desires it does not apply to an incumbent vice-president. Henry Wallace was unceremoniously dumped in 1944. And only five vice-presidents have received renomination since 1856: Republicans Sherman (1912), Curtis (1932), and Nixon (1956), and Democrats Marshall (1916) and Garner (1936).

"As an officer of the Government, the Vice-President is completely powerless," says a man who spent almost 40 years in Congress, two-term Vice-President John N. Garner. Yet because the vice-president succeeds to the presidency on the death of the president, his selection is an important convention function. Seven times out of 33 the vice-president has become chief executive by reason of the death of the president. Not since a president died in office in 1841 has the country had as many as four presidents in succession without having one elevated from the vice-presidency. More than a quarter of this time, the nation has been led by men who were originally elected as vice-presidents. Yet how seriously did the conventions consider the merits of the seven men who became "president-by-chance"?

Senator John Tyler of Virginia, selected as William Henry Harrison's running mate on the Whig ticket in 1840, was nominated primarily to attract anti-Jackson and pro-Calhoun votes away from the Democrats in the South. The next president-by-accident, Millard Fillmore, was Zachary Taylor's running mate in 1848. Being a New Yorker, he was put on the ballot to help swing that pivotal state.

Presidents Harrison and Taylor, who both died in office, were the only two Whigs elected. Perhaps if that party had taken more care in the selection of vice-presidential candidates, it would have had a longer life span. Both Tyler and Fillmore abandoned the party, and the Whigs passed into history in the early 1850's.

An assassin's bullet lifted Andrew Johnson to the presidency. Johnson was a southern War Democrat from Tennessee. In 1864 the Republican party dropped Hannibal Hamlin, Lincoln's first running mate, in a move designed to strengthen the ticket by presenting a "united front" during the Civil War. But taking a vice-presidential candidate from the opposition party had serious ramifications later when

Johnson, the Democrat elected by Republicans, locked horns with a Republican Congress.

The next vice-president to succeed to the presidency, Chester A. Arthur, was nominated with James Garfield at the Republican convention of 1880. Arthur's claim to fame was that he had served with little distinction as collector of customs for the Port of New York. However, he belonged to a group of Republicans known as "Stalwarts," who were supporters of Grant. They were engaged in a bitter controversy with a branch of the party called "Half Breeds," and Arthur's nomination was intended to heal this factional fight and give a facade of harmony.

When William McKinley was assassinated at the Buffalo Exposition in 1901, Theodore Roosevelt was elevated to the White House. The 1900 Republican convention chose Roosevelt as vice-presidential candidate in large part because Tom Platt, political boss in New York, wanted to get rid of him. Governor Roosevelt was too difficult for Platt to handle, and so he "buried" him in the vice-presidency. Platt's shrewd strategy completely outfoxed cagey Republican National Chairman Mark Hanna, who in his desperation to block Roosevelt angrily blustered, "Don't any of you realize that there's only one life between this madman and the White House?"

The next succession of a vice-president came with

the death of Warren G. Harding in 1923. His vice-president, Calvin Coolidge, was nominated in 1920 when the convention revolted against the senatorial cabal that had engineered the Harding nomination. Actually, the candidate who was slated to be on the ticket was Senator Irving Lenroot of Wisconsin. But the convention suddenly resisted dictation and picked instead "Silent Cal," an easterner from Massachusetts, whose reputation in handling a Boston police strike was a major factor in his being chosen.

The last case of vice-presidential succession occurred in 1945, when Harry S. Truman became chief executive. Truman gained national recognition for his work as chairman of a Senate investigating committee during World War II. There are many theories about Truman's victory at the 1944 Democratic convention. Part of the confusion stems from a letter of President Roosevelt stating, "I would personally vote for [Henry Wallace] if I were a delegate. . . ." However, it is agreed that this was window-dressing. James F. Byrnes writes that he had been the President's first choice, but that Ed Flynn and labor leader Sidney Hillman persuaded F.D.R. to switch to Truman. It appears certain, however, that Truman won for the same reason that most vice-presidential candidates are put on the ticket— he was the presidential nominee's choice.

When General Eisenhower was asked by reporters how Nixon happened to be picked in 1952, he ex-

Thomas Platt, political boss of the Republican Party in New York State, shrewdly engineered the vice presidential nomination of Governor Theodore Roosevelt in 1900.

plained that after his own nomination he wrote down five names that he considered acceptable. The party leaders then conferred and decided upon Senator Nixon of California.

The opinion of the presidential nominee is always the most important influence in the selection of the vice-president. When the candidate for president fails to indicate a preference, a fight often develops over the nomination. In 1868, Grant, the Republican nominee, took no hand in the selection of the vice-presidential candidate; the convention went five ballots before nominating Schuyler Colfax. Bryan, the Democratic nominee in 1896, played no part in selecting his running mate, and again it took five ballots before agreement was reached. Most recently, at the 1956 Democratic convention, presidential candidate Stevenson's refusal to state his choice triggered a fight over the vice-presidential nomination.

One problem of the past may not plague future conventions. That is the great difficulty in getting able men to run for the vice-presidency. When Daniel Webster was offered a vice-presidential nomination in 1840, he told Thurlow Weed, an important political chieftain: "No thank you, I do not propose to be buried until I am really dead and in my coffin." In 1920, when Hiram Johnson of California was approached to run for vice-president with Harding, it is said that he replied, "We're living in a day of strange events, but none so strange as that

I should be considered second to Senator Harding."
Frank Lowden was nominated for vice-president by
the 1924 Republican convention and promptly refused to run. And John C. Calhoun, an able southern statesman, resigned the vice-presidency to return to the Senate. To him, serving as a senator from
South Carolina was more important than being vice-
president of the United States.

Whatever their disclaimers, of course, the lesson
of Levi P. Morton is probably a matter of "agonizing
reappraisal" for all who are considered vice-presidential timber. Rejecting the second place nomination in 1880, Morton lived to see his proposed running mate, James Garfield, elected President and die
in office at the hand of an assassin.

One vice-presidential candidate's chief qualification was that he had a famous relative—the Democrats picked William Jennings Bryan's brother in
1924. That day is past. Today, the nation concurs
with Adlai Stevenson, who told the 1956 Democratic convention: "The responsibilities of the Presidency have grown so great that the nation's attention never before has been so focused on the Vice-
President. The choice is almost as great as the choice
of the Presidency."

In 1924, "The Great Commoner," William Jennings Bryan, still had enough power in Democratic circles to get the vice presidential nomination for his brother Charles, Governor of Nebraska.

☆ ☆ ☆ *The Monday Morning Quarterback*

For many, the fun begins after the game is over. And the presidential nominating convention is as fair game for the Monday Morning Quarterback as any Rose Bowl.

One species of convention armchair general is the "atmospheric critic." Contending that serious business is best conducted in a somber atmosphere, he confuses glumness with profundity. Americans have a tradition of mixing general horseplay with politics, and, fortunately, there is no cause to believe that a sense of humor unduly corrupts the important business of the convention. The convention has become a circus, but, in the words of Alistair Cooke, it is a "chess tournament disguised as a circus."

An appraisal of the presidential convention must come to grips with two questions: (1) Is the system representative? (2) Does it produce the best possible candidates?

There is, of course, a distinct difference between the decisions made in the nominating convention and in the general election. The convention is a party matter. It must be representative of the political party alone.

A party doesn't reform; it is reformed. When abuses become gross, it is then forced to make changes. Through bitter experience, the parties have made adjustments in the distribution of convention votes to reflect the party's strength on a state, regional, and sectional basis. Yet at the 1956 Democratic convention the small state of Nevada had 11 delegates for each 25,000 votes cast in the state for Stevenson in 1952, while New York had fewer than one delegate per 25,000 votes. Changes are still needed, but at least we have corrected some of the worst abuses of malapportionment.

However, in the important convention committees, each state, regardless of size or political leaning, has the same voice. This situation, in which an identical line-up of states in committee and on the convention floor can produce opposite results, encourages floor fights and is hardly a healthy condition for the parties. The solution would seem to be a revised representation on the committees to mirror the voting makeup of the full convention.

Another facet of representation is the degree to which the delegates are representative of the party rank and file. Toward the end of the century, a Cook County, Illinois, political convention was made up of 723 delegates, of whom 17 had been tried for homicide, 46 had been in penitentiaries for homicide or other felonies, 84 were known to have criminal records, one-third were saloonkeepers, and several others were identified as gamblers or operators of houses of prostitution.

Today the best studies on delegates to presidential conventions indicate that they have a higher than average income and educational level. If not typical of their constituents, at least they differ on the side of greater ability to meet the challenge of convention decisions.

Assuming that all the delegates are of an exceptionally high competence, the manner in which they are selected is still of great importance—means rarely justify ends. Does the party rank and file have sufficient opportunity in the delegate-selection process? Is the process consistent with our democratic tradition?

Commenting on the delegates to an early Democratic convention, the distinguished South Carolina statesman John C. Calhoun said: "Instead, then, of being directly or fresh from the people, the delegates to the Baltimore convention will be delegates of delegates, and of course removed, in all cases, at least three, if not four degrees from the people. At each successive remove, the voice of the people will become less full and distinct, until at last it will be so faint and imperfect as not to be audible."

This condition later gave rise to the primary system of selecting convention delegates. Yet, while the primaries have failed to be the cure-all, we have been slow to admit their serious frailties. Few have dared question whether the primary has fatal weakness for party responsibility.

Fantastic claims were once made for primary elections. For example, in 1898, the noted economist John R. Commons argued that a primary-election law would "increase the devotion to party and the acquiescence of the minority in the leadership of the majority." Mustering the wisdom of hindsight, no experience with primaries suggests this. Rather, one is tempted to conclude that the primaries have almost the opposite effect.

Of the 18 presidential primaries in 1956, the two declared candidates in the Democratic party sought a direct contest only in Minnesota, California, and Florida. And the true rank-and-file sentiment was blurred in two of these states—by the possibility of cross-voting in Minnesota, and by the peculiar situation in Florida, where thousands who regularly vote Republican in national elections are registered as Democrats in order to have a voice in state political affairs.

Too often primaries have been used not positively as a measure of men, but negatively to eliminate opponents. An unusual instance of this was a 1952 scheme aimed at cutting down the strength of Eisenhower in the Oregon presidential primary. Some followers of Taft, without his consent, filed Wayne Morse in the primary, also without Morse's consent. This created a ridiculous situation in which Senator Morse was compelled to barnstorm about the state urging voters *not* to vote for him. It reputedly cost Morse $10,000 to campaign against himself.

The ineffectiveness of the primaries is shown by the dismal record of primary winners at the conventions. Teddy Roosevelt had an impressive string of primary victories in 1912, but lost the nomination. Senator Albert Cummins in 1916 and Senator Hiram Johnson in 1920, came out on top of the primaries, but trailed badly at the Republican conventions. Furthermore, the candidates to run in the most primaries in recent years, Harold Stassen and Estes Kefauver, also ran out of steam by the final ballot.

Moreover, there is something degrading and wasteful about a future president running in and out of soda fountains, beauty parlors, and chain stores, flushing votes after the fashion of a county commissioner working over his own precinct.

The alternative to primaries is, of course, the older system of selecting delegates by convention. Based on the assumption that those who do the work and take the interest in party affairs should choose the delegates, the convention method makes it more difficult for the casually interested to participate in the selection of delegates. Yet it does not exclude them, for one need only inquire to discover the extent to which most political organizations are "open shops." Only an active citizenry can reverse Arthur Krock's observation that "state conventions can be boss-ruled more easily than state primaries, and often are."

Abandoning the selection of delegates by convention has an adverse effect upon the organizational vitality of a minority party. This cannot be taken lightly; if the function of the party out of power is to develop leadership for that day when it is brought to power, it is important to encourage the best means to preserve its vitality. And the convention, not the primary, seems particularly useful in this respect.

Some of the confusion about presidential primaries today is that they occur at different times and without any unifying force. Would this be eliminated by a national primary? Thomas Dewey, twice a presidential nominee, thinks this would just compound the problem:

> . . . Who could possibly run in ten or twenty primaries, to say nothing of (fifty)? Nobody could stand the physical strain of such widespread travel and continuous speaking.
>
> Moreover, no candidate could possibly devote himself so exclusively to the pursuit of the Presidency unless he were either very wealthy or unemployed. Certainly, no one holding responsible office either in the Congress or as a Governor of a state could ever again be nominated for President under such a system.
>
> The expense would also be prohibitive. The cost to each candidate would run into many millions of dollars and if such sums could be raised, which I doubt, their expenditure would create a public revulsion.

A national primary too would deprive our political parties of their greatest deliberative function. For the national convention brings the party rank and file and leadership into an interaction that is important in the competition for the mind of the party as well as for its body. Certainly the convention is essential to carbonate organizational efforts, particularly in the lean years, when a party may be fated to be out of power for several elections. It must not be overlooked that the convention serves as a meeting ground for the "business agents" of a vast nationwide organization. Although this may have nothing to do with selecting candidates, the opportunity for leaders from all parts of the country to come together, exchange information, and write party policy, is a valuable contribution that the convention makes to our political life.

Broadly then, we answer affirmatively the question, "Is the presidential nominating system representative?" Changes have raised the caliber of the delegate and the equity of apportionment. Changes are still very much needed to tighten primary laws that weaken party responsibility and to encourage the rank and file to participate in the selection of delegates by the local convention method.

Whether the convention produces the best possible candidate is difficult to assess because there is often a great deal of difference between a candidate and a president. Candidates with unexceptional records have turned into extremely adequate presidents. A system that relies heavily in picking candidates on factors that are unrelated to ability has managed to come up with a very high percentage of able men. Even the "also rans" have generally had an unmistakable luster, as seen when the losing candidates since 1916 pass in review: Charles Evans Hughes . . . James M. Cox . . . John W. Davis . . . Alfred E. Smith . . . Herbert Hoover . . . Alfred Landon . . . Wendell Willkie . . . Thomas E. Dewey . . . Adlai E. Stevenson.

We have little cause for complacency, however, in our selection of vice-presidential candidates, although the seven who succeeded to the presidency did a creditable job and three were later elected on their own. Perhaps fortune has favored us. Who would have thought Chester Arthur would make an acceptable president?

There have been many proposals for changing the system of vice-presidential selection. One suggests that the nominee for vice-president be chosen *before* the presidential candidate. It is argued that the delegates would act more responsibly if the atmosphere in which the running mate is picked were not so anticlimactic and if they were not so tired and anxious to get home.

Other proposals call for the vice-presidential nominee to be chosen from the top three contenders for the presidential nomination; for presidential and vice-presidential candidates to seek the nomination as a team; for the duties of the vice-president to be increased so as to tease better-qualified people into the race for the nomination; to decrease the duties of the office, relieving the vice-president of the responsibility of presiding over the Senate, allowing him to retain another job (such as senator or governor), with the one vice-presidential function being to succeed to the presidency if it becomes necessary.

Certainly the most powerful catalytic agent to speed up changes in convention procedure and man-

agement has been the television camera. **Right before** the 1952 Democratic convention, National
Chairman Frank E. McKinney said:

> People tell me that this Convention and the
> Republican Convention will be viewed by the
> largest viewing audience in the history of any po-
> litical convention. Namely, about 60 million peo-
> ple. Therefore it behooves us to make this as in-
> teresting as possible. We're going to attempt to
> restrict the nominating and seconding speeches to
> the shortest period of time possible, and to dis-
> courage as much as possible the demonstrations,
> such as parades.

By 1956, three quarters of the population had television sets available. Leo Bogart reports, in *The Age
of Decision,* that 93% of the television families spent
an estimated average of over 16 hours per home following the conventions. Like any other television
show, the convention producers watch their ratings
and listen to audience reaction. What isn't popular
with the public is likely to be changed in the future.

But television and other coverage of the convention has a more beneficial effect than merely elimi-
nating some tedium. The televised convention is
hardly the place to be caught with your hand in
someone else's pocket. For example, the manner in
which the New York Democratic convention in
Buffalo picked its 1956 candidate for the Senate may
have caused enough public reaction to affect the out-

come of the election that followed. The frailties of the convention are basically those of men, not of institutions. While there have been no signs of corruption in national conventions in recent years, the public gaze now encourages added honesty.

The inescapable conclusion is that the national presidential nominating system has proved itself because it has met the basic political test—it works. It gives the United States an orderly method of leadership succession. It may be completely unintelligible to outsiders—the usually astute foreign observer of our government, M. Ostrogorski, threw up his hands and concluded, "God takes care of drunkards, of little children, and of the United States!" There are, of course, also those who believe that democratic decisions should be made by uprighteous Univac; that we can attain the millennium by building into our political system some kind of institution that will mirror every nuance of public opinion. The nominating convention is clearly not such a mechanism. It is made up of men and women; of human virtue and error. Yet through this fallible machinery, the American people are given a free choice for president. When the campaign heat cools, the brickbats stop flying, the smoke lifts, we can be sure that the nation will unite behind its chief executive. This is the greatest tribute we can pay the presidential nominating system.

Appendix—Major Party Presidential Candidates, 1856-1956

Republicans	*Democrats*

1856

JOHN C. FRÉMONT (CALIF.)	JAMES BUCHANAN (PA.)
Age when nominated: 43	Age when nominated: 65
Ballot nominated: 1st	Ballot nominated: 17th
Place of nomination: Philadelphia	Place of nomination: Cincinnati
Nickname: The Pathfinder	Nickname: Old Fogey, Old Public Functionary
Background: Army Officer Explorer U. S. Senator	Background: Diplomat Secretary of State U. S. Senator Member House of Representatives State legislator

Republicans	*Democrats*
	1860	

ABRAHAM LINCOLN (ILL.)	STEPHEN A. DOUGLAS (ILL.)
Age when nominated: 51	Age when nominated: 47
Ballot nominated: 3d	Ballot nominated: 59th*
Place of nomination: Chicago	Place of nomination: Baltimore*
Nickname: The Rail Splitter, Father Abraham	Nickname: The Little Giant
Background:	Background:
Member, House of Representatives	U. S. Senator
Lawyer	Member, House of Representatives
State legislator	State legislator
	Lawyer

1864

ABRAHAM LINCOLN	GEORGE B. MC CLELLAN (N. J.)
Incumbent	Age when nominated: 38
Ballot nominated: 1st	Ballot nominated: 1st
Place of nomination: Baltimore	Place of nomination: Chicago
	Nickname: Little Mac
	Background:
	Army General
	Engineer

* The convention met in Charleston and adjourned after 57 ballots without reaching agreement. It reconvened in Baltimore, nominating Douglas on the 2nd ballot.

Republicans	Democrats

1868

ULYSSES S. GRANT (ILL.)
Age when nominated: 46
Ballot nominated: 1st
Place of nomination: Chicago
Nickname: The Hero of Appomattox
Background:
  Army General

HORATIO SEYMOUR (N. Y.)
Age when nominated: 58
Ballot nominated: 22d
Place of nomination: New York
Background:
  Governor
  Lawyer

1872

ULYSSES S. GRANT
Incumbent
Ballot nominated: 1st
Place of nomination:
  Philadelphia

HORACE GREELEY (N. Y.)
Age when nominated: 61
Ballot nominated: 1st
Place of nomination: Baltimore
Nickname: Old White Hat
Background:
  Newspaper publisher
    and editor
  Member, House of Representatives

1876

RUTHERFORD B. HAYES (OHIO)
Age when nominated: 54
Ballot nominated: 7th
Place of nomination: Cincinnati

SAMUEL J. TILDEN (N. Y.)
Age when nominated: 62
Ballot nominated: 2d
Place of nomination: St. Louis

Republicans	Democrats
Nickname: Old 8 to 7	Nickname: The Great Forecloser, The Sage of Greystone

Background:
  Governor
  Army General
  Member, House of Representatives
  Lawyer
	Background:
	  Governor
	  Lawyer
	  State legislator

1880

JAMES A. GARFIELD (OHIO)	WINFIELD S. HANCOCK (PA.)
Age when nominated: 49	Age when nominated: 56
Ballot nominated: 36th	Ballot nominated: 2d
Place of nomination: Chicago	Place of nomination: Cincinnati
Nickname: Canal Boy	Nickname: Superb Hancock

Background:
  Member, House of Representatives
  Army General
  Lawyer
  Educator
  State legislator
	Background:
	  Army General

1884

JAMES G. BLAINE (MAINE)	GROVER CLEVELAND (N. Y.)
Age when nominated: 54	Age when nominated: 47
Ballot nominated: 4th	Ballot nominated: 2d
Place of nomination: Chicago	Place of nomination: Chicago

Republicans

Nickname: The Plumed
   Knight, The Continen-
   tal Liar from the State
   of Maine, The Mag-
   netic Statesman, The
   Tattooed Man
Background:
   Secretary of State
   Speaker of the House
      of Representatives
   U. S. Senator
   Teacher
   Editor
   State legislator

Democrats

Nickname: The Hangman
   of Buffalo
Background:
   Governor
   Mayor
   Lawyer

1888

BENJAMIN HARRISON
(OHIO)
Age when nominated: 55
Ballot nominated: 8th
Place of nomination: Chi-
   cago
Nickname: Kid Glove
   Harrison
Background:
   U. S. Senator
   Lawyer
   Army General

GROVER CLEVELAND

Incumbent
Ballot nominated: 1st
Place of nomination: St.
   Louis

1892

BENJAMIN HARRISON
Incumbent

GROVER CLEVELAND
Ex-President

Republicans	*Democrats*
Ballot nominated: 1st	Ballot nominated: 1st
Place of nomination: Minneapolis	Place of nomination: Chicago

1896

WILLIAM MC KINLEY, JR. (OHIO)	WILLIAM JENNINGS BRYAN (NEBR.)
Age when nominated: 53	Age when nominated: 36
Ballot nominated: 1st	Ballot nominated: 5th
Place of nomination: St. Louis	Place of nomination: Chicago
Nickname: Idol of Ohio, Napoleon of Protection	Nickname: The Boy Orator of the Platte, The Great Commoner, The Peerless Leader
Background: Governor	Background:
Member, House of Representatives	Member, House of Representatives
Army officer	Lawyer
Lawyer	

1900

WILLIAM MC KINLEY, JR.	WILLIAM JENNINGS BRYAN
Incumbent	See 1896
Ballot nominated: 1st	Ballot nominated: 1st
Place of nomination: Philadelphia	Place of nomination: Kansas City

1904

THEODORE ROOSEVELT (N. Y.)	ALTON B. PARKER (N. Y.)
Age when nominated: 46	Age when nominated: 52

Republicans	Democrats
Ballot nominated: 1st	Ballot nominated: 1st
Place of nomination: Chicago	Place of nomination: St. Louis
Nickname: Cowboy President, The Hero of San Juan Hill, The Roughrider	Nickname: The Gold Candidate
Background:	Background:
President	Judge
Vice-President	
Governor	
Military Officer	
Asst. Secy. of Navy	
Civil Service Commissioner	
Police Commissioner	
State legislator	

1908

WILLIAM HOWARD TAFT (OHIO)	WILLIAM JENNINGS BRYAN
Age when nominated: 51	Twice defeated candidate for President
Ballot nominated: 1st	Ballot nominated: 1st
Place of nomination: Chicago	Place of nomination: Denver
Background:	
Secretary of War	
Judge	
Solicitor General	
Governor of the Philippines	

Republicans	*Democrats*

1912

WILLIAM HOWARD TAFT	WOODROW WILSON (N. J.)
Incumbent	Age when nominated: 56
Ballot nominated: 1st	Ballot nominated: 46th
Place of nomination: Chicago	Place of nomination: Baltimore
	Nickname: Phrasemaker, Professor
	Background:
	Governor
	University President
	Professor

1916

CHARLES EVANS HUGHES (N. Y.)	WOODROW WILSON
Age when nominated: 54	Incumbent
Ballot nominated: 3d	Ballot nominated: 1st
Place of nomination: Chicago	Place of nomination: St. Louis
Background:	
Supreme Court Justice	
Governor	

1920

WARREN G. HARDING (OHIO)	JAMES M. COX (OHIO)
Age when nominated: 55	Age when nominated: 50
Ballot nominated: 10th	Ballot nominated: 44th
Place of nomination: Chicago	Place of nomination: San Francisco
Background:	Background:
U. S. Senator	Governor

Republicans	Democrats
Newspaper publisher & editor	Newspaper publisher
State legislator	Member, House of Representatives

1924

CALVIN COOLIDGE (MASS.)	JOHN W. DAVIS (W. VA.)
Age when nominated: 52	Age when nominated: 51
Ballot nominated: 1st	Ballot nominated: 103d
Place of nomination: Cleveland	Place of nomination: New York
Nickname: Silent Cal	
Background:	Background:
President	Diplomat
Vice-President	Solicitor General
Governor	Member, House of Representatives
State legislator	
Lawyer	

1928

HERBERT HOOVER (CALIF.)	ALFRED E. SMITH (N. Y.)
Age when nominated: 54	Age when nominated: 55
Ballot nominated: 1st	Ballot nominated: 1st
Place of nomination: Kansas City	Place of nomination: Houston
Nickname: Chief	Nickname: The Happy Warrior
Background:	Background:
Secretary of Commerce	Governor
Engineer	State legislator
Food Administrator (World War I)	

Republicans	Democrats

1932

HERBERT HOOVER	FRANKLIN D. ROOSEVELT
Incumbent	(N. Y.)
	Age when nominated: 50
Ballot nominated: 1st	Ballot nominated: 4th
Place of nomination: Chi-cago	Place of nomination: Chi-cago
	Nickname: F.D.R.
	Background:
	Governor
	Asst. Secy. of Navy
	State legislator
	Lawyer

1936

ALFRED M. LANDON	FRANKLIN D. ROOSEVELT
(KAN.)	Incumbent
Age when nominated: 45	
Ballot nominated: 1st	Ballot nominated: 1st
Place of nomination: Cleveland	Place of nomination: Phil-adelphia
Nickname: The Kansas Coolidge	
Background:	
Governor	
Businessman	

1940

WENDELL L. WILLKIE	FRANKLIN D. ROOSEVELT
(N. ,Y.)	
Age when nominated: 48	Incumbent

Republicans

Ballot nominated: 6th
Place of nomination:
  Philadelphia
Nickname: The Barefoot
  Boy from Wall Street
Background:
  Businessman
  Lawyer

Democrats

Ballot nominated: 1st
Place of nomination: Chi-
  cago

1944

THOMAS E. DEWEY (N. Y.)
Age when nominated: 42
Ballot nominated: 1st
Place of nomination: Chi-
  cago
Background:
  Governor
  District Attorney

FRANKLIN D. ROOSEVELT
Incumbent
Ballot nominated: 1st
Place of nomination: Chi-
  cago

1948

THOMAS E. DEWEY
See 1944
Ballot nominated: 3d
Place of nomination:
  Philadelphia

HARRY S. TRUMAN (MO.)
Age when nominated: 64
Ballot nominated: 1st
Place of nomination: Phil-
  adelphia
Nickname: Man from In-
  dependence, Man from
  Missouri
Background:
  President
  Vice-President
  U. S. Senator

Republicans	*Democrats*

1952

DWIGHT D. EISENHOWER (N. Y.)	ADLAI E. STEVENSON (ILL.)
Age when nominated: 62	Age when nominated: 52
Ballot nominated: 1st	Ballot nominated: 3d
Place of nomination: Chicago	Place of nomination: Chicago
Nickname: Ike	
Background:	Background:
Army General	Governor
University President	Lawyer

1956

DWIGHT D. EISENHOWER (PA).	ADLAI E. STEVENSON
Incumbent	See 1952
Ballot nominated: 1st	
Place of nomination: San Francisco	Ballot nominated: 1st
	Place of nomination: Chicago

☆ ☆ ☆ *Index*

Bronx County, 80
Brookings Institution, 113-114, 114-115
Brown, B. Gratz, 145
Brown, Charles, 85
Browning, Gordon, 139
Bryan, Charles W., 158
Bryan, William Jennings, 42, 48, 105-106, 145, 157; youngest presidential candidate, 50; "Dark Horse" nomination of, 54-57; wins three nominations, 62; supports Wilson in 1912, 65; background of, 178
Bryce, Lord James, on presidency, 40
Byrnes, James F., 154
Buchanan, James, 35, 48, 50; background of, 173
Buffalo, 153, 170, 177
"Bull Moose" Party, see Progressive Party of 1912
Burke, Edmund, 80
Burkhardt, Robert J., 83
Burr, Aaron, 143
Businessmen, 182, 183; as potential candidates, 45; as convention delegates, 116
Butler, Paul M., 68, 117

Cabinet, presidential, 45; presidential candidates who served in, 173, 177, 179, 181
Calhoun, John Caldwell, 152, 158; on convention delegates, 163-164
California, 41, 57, 66-67, 83, 147, 157, 173; electoral vote of, 47; population increase of, 49; 1956 primary in, 88, 164; national conventions in, 68, 180, 184
Call, convention, 68
Cass, Lewis, 35, 53, 137
Catholic, 68; as "availability" factor, 49-50; convention delegates, 115
Caucus; Congressional, 20;

precinct, 85; national convention delegation, 135
Chairman, delegation, 21, 123, 129, 130-131
Chairman, national committee, 67-69, 98
Chairman, national convention permanent, 23, 78, 123, 133, 138; selection of, 106-109
Chairman, national convention temporary; selection of, 69; as keynoter, 119
Charleston, 174
Chicago, 70, 73, 74, 84, 85, 92, 116; conventions at, 31, 105, 140, 174, 175, 176-177, 178, 179, 180, 182, 182-183, 184
Chicago *Tribune*, 70
Cincinnati; conventions at, 137, 173, 175, 176
"Citizens for Eisenhower," 43
Civil Service, 114
Civil War, 32, 36, 48, 73, 124, 152
Clark, Champ, 135
Clay, Henry, 35, 42
Cleveland (city), 31; convention at, 70, 182
Cleveland, Grover, 26, 35, 39, 48, 146; nominated, 52; renominated, 65; opposed by Tammany Hall, 132; background of, 176-177
Cobb, Irvin; on conventions, 18
Colfax, Schuyler, 144, 157
Colorado, 46, 105
Columbia University, 47
Commons, John R, 164
Commonwealth and Southern Co., 43
Congress of Industrial Organizations (C.I.O.), 115
Congress of the United States, see House of Representatives, United States, *and* Senate, United States
Connally, Thomas, 134
Connecticut, 40, 115, 131
Constitution, United States;